RETURN TO THE SOURCE

RETURN
TO THE
SOURCE

Collected Writings on Spiritual Life

Swami Bhajanananda Saraswati

Foreword by
Swami Ambikananda Saraswati

Return to the Source
Second Edition 2016

ISBN-13: 978-1523687701
ISBN-10: 1523687703

Published by Kali Mandir
Ramakrishna Ashrama
P.O. Box 4700
Laguna Beach, CA 92651
www.kalimandir.org

Design and Production by: Naren K. Schreiner
Cover design: Janzel Martinez
Cover photo: The author and Swami Vishwatmananda, head of Ramakrishna
Kutir in Amarkantak, India, by Ritika Guha of Creative Guilds Photography
www.creativeguilds.com

Dedicated to Sri Ramakrishna Paramahamsa, the
great world teacher and incarnation of divinity who
taught the transcendent unity of religion, the
motherhood of God and the mystical path of love.

আহা কি সুন্দর স্থান! কি সুন্দর মানুষ!
কি সুন্দর কথা! এখান থেকে নড়তে ইচ্ছা করছে না!

*Ah! What a beautiful place! What a beautiful man!
What beautiful words! I don't want to move from here!*

~ Sri M.

Acknowledgments

I am happy to mention my debt of appreciation to my friends and well-wishers who have helped in so many ways to bring this book to production, especially: Swami Ambikananda Saraswati for his beautiful foreword; Daya Avshman for combing social media to save my words from the darkness of the cyber-void; Debra Shwiff for her hours of proofreading; and Kamalakanta (Naren K. Schreiner, director of Sangita Yoga), for his tireless work in designing, formatting and producing the book.

I would also like to thank Nandikesha (Janzel Martinez) for his help with the cover design; Swami Mahayogananda for his help with some Sanskrit questions; Ritika Guha for permission to use her incredible photograph on the front cover; and Elizabeth Usha Harding for her support throughout.

Grateful acknowledgments for permission to reprint short selections from their publications are due to Vedanta Society of St. Louis; Udbodhan, Kolkata; Ramakrishna Math, Chennai; Advaita Ashrama, Kolkata; Ramakrishna Math, Bangalore; and Divine Life Society, Rishikesh. Full references are included in footnotes.

Finally, I express my gratitude for the kind words that appear on the back cover, written by Rev. Swami Chetananandaji Maharaj, senior monk of the Ramakrishna Math and Mission and head of the Vedanta Society of St. Louis; Dr. Layne R. Little, lecturer in Religious Studies at the University of California, Berkeley; and our very dear Rampriya Das (Trevor Hall).

Contents

Foreword
By Swami Ambikananda Saraswati xi
Preface xv
Thakur's Prayer xx

1. Sri Ramakrishna and Kali in the West 1

2. Kali Puja
The Art of Seeing God 19

3. Kirtan
Singing the Divine Name 35

4. Japa Yoga 45

5. Moment by Moment Worship 57

6. Bhagavatam Meditations 63

7. Tradition
Gift of the Rishis 71

8. The Seeds of Desire 85

9. Return to the Source
Excerpts from Letters to Devotees 89

Foreword

If we were to open up all the scriptures of the Hindu tradition and spread them before us, we would find, nestled among a theological diversity unparalleled in the history of religious thought, a subtle commonality, a simple thread running through the core of each of them, binding them together. Whether it is Sri Krishna and Arjuna or Sukadev and Parikshit, Yama Raj and Nachiketas or Yajnavalkya and Maitreyi, Kakbushundi and Garuda or Sri Ramakrishna and Mahendranath Gupta—we find that each of these scriptures, at its heart, is simply a disciple sitting next to a guru, asking a question and receiving an answer. Indeed, the word "*upanishad*" literally means "to sit near."

But even that dynamic between guru and disciple, that sitting near, that questioning and responding, is but a manifestation or expression of an even subtler dynamic. The essence of spiritual life itself is the interplay between two forces: a seeker's sincerity and a divine grace. These two forces meet—spiritually, philosophically, and practically—in the person of the guru.

And, of course, every true guru was, is, and always will be, a disciple. Every guru was once sitting near and questioning. And the answers have their source. A *sampradaya* (initiatic lineage) is a river of divine grace, whose ancient waters still flow without ceasing, and from whose waters each new disciple draws to quench the deepest of thirsts. *Return to the Source* is a view of one such river, a chance for us to sit near and witness these dynamics in action.

Swami Bhajanananda Saraswati is a disciple of the great yogi, Swami Vishnudevananda Saraswati of Prayag (1904-1997), and received *sannyas* from his successor, Swami Omananda Saraswati. This present collection of writings are, in part, Swami Bhajanananda's articulations of spiritual instructions he received from them, instructions which earlier had been passed on by Yogiraj Handiya Baba (1850-1954).

And so on. We can follow this river of grace back through the ages. We can hear the echoes of a question from antiquity that is still just as relevant and full of urgency for us who are here today, downstream, as it was for that ancient questioner. But also as the river flows, new waters mingle. And as these traditional matters of principle and practice enter the modern world, their contexts shift. Along the banks of the river the landscape changes, creating challenges utterly unique to our 21st-century minds.

So in addition to being an expression of grace received through initiation and tradition, *Return to the Source* also represents Swami Bhajananananda's personal response, as a sadhu, to these new sets of challenges that confront us. Some of these writings were originally his replies to specific questions sent via email or social media. Some were originally articles commissioned by magazines or journals. Some appeared as posts on his Cyber Dhuni blog. Some were his spoken remarks that were written down by the listener the old-fashioned way, with pen to paper.

But still the essence is there throughout: a sincere search, honest answers. These writings have been edited and loosely arranged by topic, which range from the practical constituents of singing kirtan, chanting japa or wearing a kaupina, to descriptions of the mystical underpinnings of traditional puja or yogasanas, to his meditations on verses from the *Srimad Bhagavatam* or *Devi Mahatmyam*. There are also personal self-reflective moments which in their honesty instruct as they reveal.

It will not take long for the reader to discover among these writings an over-arching presence: that of Sri Ramakrishna Paramahamsa. His words of nectar, perhaps more than anything else, have been Swami Bhajanananda's source of solace and inspiration. Sri Ramakrishna's simple words shatter a million doubts, his holy life embodies a grace that floods the heart with a deep yearning for the divine. His was a life of purest ecstasy, and the reader will find his words and his life referred to again and again within these pages.

And with Sri Ramakrishna there is always Mother Kali. As a devotee of Kali, Swami Bhajanananda aspires to live a pure life at Her feet, and the reader will find within the present volume many invaluable insights and inspirations regarding this all-too-often misunderstood Dark Mother.

Swami Bhajanananda lives in the Ramakrishna Ashrama at Kali Mandir in Laguna Beach, California. As a monastic pujari, he serves the awakened deity of Ma Dakshineswari Kali and Her devotees. It should be noted that since Kali Mandir has no official guru,

Return to the Source is being published not as a collection of official directives or instructions for devotees, but rather as a source of inspiration, as an example of traditional wisdom in this age of modern dilemmas, as an opportunity for us to read the words of a sincere sadhu. It is as we said before: a chance for us to come close to the river and "sit near".

Swami Ambikananda Saraswati
Nag Panchami (August 19th), 2015

Preface

The title of this small book, *Return to the Source*, refers to living consciously in the presence of God. The path shown by the saints is the path back home, the path to the realization that we have never left the womb of the Divine Mother. She is our source, our substratum and our destiny.

Although the words in this book are my own, I have tried to faithfully share the voice of tradition, the revelations of the scriptures and the teachings of my gurus. The larger Hindu tradition is vast and multifaceted and I understand that my perspective is just that—my perspective. It is my sincere hope that what has inspired me might be helpful to others walking the spiritual path.

All proceeds from the sale of this book go directly to provide food, lodging and education for the children cared for by my guru's ashram, the Yoga Vedanta Kutir in Allahabad, India.

Swami Bhajanananda Saraswati
Makar Sankranti (January 14th), 2016

Swami Bhajanananda Saraswati in front of his kutir
at Kali Mandir Ramakrishna Ashrama.

Swami Omananda Saraswati
Yoga Vedanta Kutir, Allahabad, India.

Brahmaleen Swami Vishnudevananda Saraswati
(1904-1997)

Yogiraj Handiya Baba
Swami Hridayananda Saraswati
(1850-1954)

Thakur's Prayer

"মা আমি তোমার শরণাগত, শরণাগত! ..."

Ma, I've taken shelter of You!
I've taken shelter of You!
I've taken shelter at Your holy lotus feet.
I don't want the pleasures of the body, Ma!
I don't want people's respect!
I don't want the eight mystical powers.
Just do this: may I have pure devotion for Your holy
lotus feet—desireless, stainless, selfless devotion.
And Ma, may I not be captivated
by Your world-bewitching maya.
And in Your world of illusion
may I never have love for the objects
of lust and greed.
Ma! Except for You, I have no one else.
I'm without any worship,
without any spiritual practice,
without any knowledge,
without any devotion.
Be gracious and give me devotion
for Your holy lotus feet.[1]

~ Sri Ramakrishna Paramahamsa

---

1 *Sri Sri Ramakrishna Kathamrita*, translation by Swami Ambikananda Saraswati.

Ma Dakshineswari Kali
Kali Mandir, Laguna Beach, California.

1

Sri Ramakrishna and Kali in the West

"When you weep with intense yearning, She can be seen. People weep a bucket of tears for family; people weep a flood of tears for money; but who is weeping for God? You have to call out with a real cry. As soon as there's yearning, the dawn sky has become red. After that the Sun will show himself. After yearning is the vision of God."

~ Sri Ramakrishna Paramahamsa

Sri Ramakrishna and Kali
in the West[1]

"Sisters and brothers of America." These words changed the world. Swami Vivekananda's famous speech, given in 1893 at the Parliament of Religions in Chicago, was one of the modern world's earliest formulations of what is now known as Hinduism. Swamiji became one of the most popular speakers at the Parliament, and his success propelled him onto the American stage and then into international renown. This allowed him, along with his brother disciples and followers, to spread yoga and Vedanta in the West and to establish the dynamic work of Ramakrishna Math and Mission in the East.

But the story does not truly begin with Swamiji's stirring words at the Parliament. It does not even begin with the life of Vivekananda. The story begins with the heart of the Divine Mother responding to the crying need of the age. The story begins with Sri Ramakrishna.

Sri Ramakrishna is considered by many as the central force behind the spiritual awakening of this age. The heart yearns for an infinite love. Through his extraordinary purity and devotion and his unprecedented spiritual disciplines and experiences, Sri Ramakrishna released a spiritual current of grace, making the divine mystery accessible to all.

---

1 First published as "Vivekananda and the Worship of Kali in the West" in *Prabuddha Bharata*, January 2013.

Avatar of the Age

Sprung from the direct experience of ancient sages, Indian culture had always been rooted in spiritual truth, which pervaded daily life. Invasion after invasion by foreign looters had cost India much, but its spiritual core remained strong, its eternal foundations resilient and adaptable to the ever-changing details of history. However, when the Europeans arrived in India, they quickly realized that in order to gain control of her wealth, they had to conquer her heart and soul as well. Many lands across the globe had fallen to European colonists, not only because of military strength but because of the introduction of European diseases such as smallpox and plague, to which the local populations had no hereditary resistance. In such weakened conditions, conquest became comparatively easy. In the case of India, what was the disease that weakened society, making it possible for a handful of Europeans to control two hundred million people? It was a materialistic worldview that values wealth above people, and people above God.

At the time of Sri Ramakrishna's advent India's ancient system of education and training was disappearing. The youth brought up in an occupied land began to identify with their occupiers and to doubt the religion and traditions that, to them, had led to such subjugation. They began imitating the West and saw India's religious traditions as obstacles to their entering the modern world. But all attempts to revitalize India by destroying the traditions that had sustained her were bound to fail.

Swami Saradananda asks: "How can India, whose soul is religion, survive if her religion is not restored to life? How is it possible for the atheistic West to eradicate the religious degradation that resulted from its own materialism?"[2]

We read in the *Bhagavad Gita* that the blessed Lord incarnates in every age, when there is a decline in dharma, for the protection of the righteous and the destruction of the wicked. Devotees of Sri Ramakrishna recognize in him the latest incarnation who came to restore the soul of India in her darkest hour, to restore her ancient dignity and spiritually uplift the world.

Kali, the Mother

Born in 1836, the very year that the British system of education was adopted in India, Sri Ramakrishna grew up in an orthodox brahmin family in the village of Kamarpukur. Although only some sixty miles from the urban center of Kolkata, the seat of English colonial power, Kamarpukur was not influenced by Western culture and thought. In 1852 Sri Ramakrishna moved to Calcutta, joining his older brother Ramkumar. This move was not only across space, but across time as well, for with this move Sri Ramakrishna encountered the nineteenth century.

Two years later he accepted to officiate as a priest (*pujari*) at Rani Rasmani's newly-built Kali temple in Dakshineswar, which would become the stage of his unprecedented spiritual practices and realizations.

---

2 Swami Saradananda, *Sri Ramakrishna and His Divine Play*, trans. Swami Chetanananda (Vedanta Society of St. Louis, 2003), p. 80.

As Kali's priest he began to ask himself if the goddess he was sincerely serving was real or not. If she was real, could one experience her directly? His intense longing for the vision of Mother Kali became so great, so overwhelming, that the Mother could not keep herself hidden from him any longer. The Master related his first vision of Kali to his close disciples:

> I had a marvelous vision of the Mother and fell down unconscious.... Within me there was a steady flow of undiluted bliss that I had never before experienced, and I felt the immediate presence of the Divine Mother.[3]

Even after this beatific vision Sri Ramakrishna was not satisfied and longed to have unbroken communion with her, sometimes rolling on the ground crying, "Mother, be gracious unto me! Reveal Yourself to me!" The Master later recounted:

> Sometimes I would lose outer consciousness from that unbearable agony. Immediately after that I would see the Mother's luminous form bestowing boons and fearlessness! I used to see Her smiling, talking, consoling, or teaching me in various ways.[4]

Universal Vision

The Divine Mother also sent him teachers to initiate him into the complicated practices of Tantra, the difficult abstractions of Vedanta, the varied devotional

---

3 *Ibid.*, p. 212.
4 *Ibid.*, p. 213.

moods of Vaishnavism, and even the 'foreign' faiths of Islam and Christianity. Each he practiced with full sincerity. And the goal presented in each opened up to him as direct experience. In the heart of every tradition he saw his Mother Kali shining. Sri Ramakrishna's famous declaration "as many faiths, so many paths" (*yato mat, tato path*) was not the result of intellectual comparison or of a modern open-mindedness. It came from his own realization, a gift of Goddess Kali to the world. The Master realized that his liberal view was singularly unique. He came to understand that the Divine Mother was working through his body and mind. She is the reality that Sri Ramakrishna incarnated. It was Her message that Sri Ramakrishna revealed.

Vivekananda and Kali

Mother Kali was Sri Ramakrishna's overwhelming reality. He sang to her, had visions of her, spoke intimately to her, and heard her voice. It was only by accepting Mother Kali that Swami Vivekananda could fully accept Sri Ramakrishna and become his pure instrument. The Master had already seen Narendra's (Vivekananda's pre-monastic name) future in a vision. He understood that it was Narendra who would lead his disciples and devotees to accomplish the Mother's mission in the world. But the young Narendra, like much of young Bengal, had been swayed by the persuasive teachings of Keshab Chandra Sen and the Brahmo Samaj. The Samaj and the other socio-religious groups of the day, responded to the challenge of the West, not with atheism, but with a Christianized form of Hinduism. In their attempt to purify Hinduism of what they saw as superstition, they preached that the various deities were false, and its members even signed loyalty oaths vowing not to bow down before images. Thus Narendra's close association with Sri Ramakrishna created a great dilemma for him, for he had witnessed the Master's power, purity, and devotion, but could not accept the Hindu world that the Master lived in: a world of gods and goddesses, of "graven images," of visions and ecstasies. Swamiji later said of this time:

> How I used to hate Kali! … and all Her ways! That was the ground of my six years' fight— that I would not accept Her. … I loved him [Sri Ramakrishna], you see, and that was what held me. I saw his marvelous purity. … I felt his wonderful love. … His greatness had not dawned on me then. All that came afterwards when I had given in. At that time I thought him a brain-sick baby, always seeing visions and the rest. I hated it. And then I too had to accept Her![5]

Like many major breakthroughs in life, Swamiji's 'accepting' Kali came as the result of a personal crisis. With the death of Narendra's father, his once affluent household was thrown into deep poverty. The young Narendra, although employable and qualified, could not secure any work to relieve his family's suffering.

---

5 Sister Nivedita, *The Master as I Saw Him,* (Udbodhan, Kolkata, 2005), pp. 139-40.

He reached the point of despair. Perhaps all this was the arrangement of the Divine Mother, for in times of great need she manifests. The Swami recounts:

It occurred to me that God grants the Master's prayers, so I should ask him to pray on my behalf that my family's financial crises would be overcome. I was sure that he wouldn't refuse, for my sake. I rushed to Dakshineswar and importuned him, saying, "Sir, you must speak to the Divine Mother so that my family's financial problems can be solved."

The Master replied: "I can't make such demands. Why don't you go and ask the Mother yourself. You don't accept the Mother—that is why you have all these troubles." I replied: "I don't know the Mother. Please tell the Mother for me. You have to, or I won't let you go."

The Master said affectionately: "My boy, I've prayed many times to the Mother to remove your suffering. But She doesn't listen to my prayers because you don't care for Her. All right, today is Tuesday, a day especially sacred to Mother. Go to the temple tonight and pray. Mother will grant whatever you ask for, I promise you that. My Mother is the embodiment of Pure Consciousness, the Power of Brahman, and She has produced this universe by mere will. What can She not do, if She wishes?"

When the Master said that, I was fully convinced that all my suffering would cease as soon as I prayed to Her. I waited impatiently for night. At 9.00 p.m. the Master told me to go to the temple. On my way, I was possessed by a kind of drunkenness and began to stagger. I firmly believed that I would see the Mother and hear Her voice. I forgot everything else and became absorbed in that thought alone. When I entered the temple, I saw that the Mother was actually conscious and living, the fountainhead of infinite love and beauty. Overwhelmed with love and devotion, I bowed down to Her again and again, praying, "Mother—grant me discrimination, grant me detachment, grant me divine knowledge and devotion, grant that I may see You without obstruction, always!" My heart was filled with peace. The universe disappeared from my mind and the Mother alone occupied it completely.[6]

Two more times Sri Ramakrishna sent him back to the temple, and all three times Swamiji forgot to ask for his family's financial relief. The Master then granted that his family would not lack plain food and clothing. On Swamiji's request, that very night the Master taught him a song, which Swamiji sang until dawn:

Mother, Thou art our sole Redeemer,
Thou the support of the three gunas,
Higher than the most high.

---

6 *Sri Ramakrishna and His Divine Play,* pp. 842-3.

Thou art compassionate, I know,
Who takest away our bitter grief.
Thou art in earth, in water You;
Thou liest as the root of all.
In me, in every creature,
Thou hast Thy home;
though clothed with form,
Yet art Thou formless Reality.
Sandhya art Thou, and Gayatri;
Thou dost sustain this universe.
Mother, the Help art Thou
Of those who have no help but Thee,
O Eternal Beloved of Shiva!

The Master was so happy that he kept telling people over and over again: "Narendra has accepted the Mother Kali. That's very good, isn't it?"[7]

During the years of his training, Narendra kept asking Sri Ramakrishna for an experience of *nirvikalpa samadhi*, the complete absorption of the self in the Divine. The moment came at Kashipur, during the Master's final illness. Sri Ramakrishna was lying awake in his bed while Narendra was downstairs in another room absorbed in deep meditation. He felt as if a lamp was burning at the back of his head when his sense of individual existence drowned in the bliss of pure Being.

When he regained normal consciousness, Sri Ramakrishna told him: "Now the Mother has shown you everything. But this revelation will remain

---

7 *Ibid.*, p. 844.

under lock and key, and I will keep the key. When you have accomplished the Mother's work you will find the treasure again."[8]

Even the realization of the non-dual Brahman comes as a gift from the Divine Mother.

"Mother's Work"

Vivekananda did not often mention Sri Ramakrishna in his public talks in the West. Even less did he reveal the centrality of Mother Kali in his life and thought. He focused instead on the message of the Master by presenting the broad underlying principles of religion, lecturing on the Upanishads, and preaching "what is good for universal humanity." Though not openly preached, the swami could not keep his love for the Divine Mother hidden from his intimate disciples.

"You see," he once said, "I cannot but believe that there is somewhere a great Power that thinks of Herself as feminine, and called Kali, and Mother."[9] Upon his return to India, he started the yearly observance of Durga Puja and Kali Puja at Belur Math, along with the daily worship of Sri Ramakrishna.

Swamiji did, in fact, on occasion speak about the Mother:

Mother is the first manifestation of power and is considered a higher idea than father. With the name of Mother comes the idea of Shakti, Divine

8 M, *The Gospel of Sri Ramakrishna*, trans. Swami Nikhilananda (Ramakrishna Math, Chennai, 2002), p. 79.
9 Swami Vivekananda, *The Complete Works of Swami Vivekananda, 9 Vols.*, (Advaita Ashram, Kolkata, 1989), p. 523.

Energy and Omnipotence, just as the baby believes
its mother to be all-powerful, able to do anything.
The Divine Mother is the Kundalini ("coiled
up" power) sleeping in us; without worshiping
Her we can never know ourselves. All-merciful,
all-powerful, omnipresent are attributes of the
Divine Mother. She is the sum total of the energy
in the universe. Every manifestation of power in
the universe is "Mother." She is life, She is intelligence, She is Love. She is in the universe yet separate from it. She is a person, and can be seen and
known (as Sri Ramakrishna saw and knew Her).
Established in the idea of Mother, we can do anything. She quickly answers prayers. She can show
Herself to us in any form at any moment. Divine
Mother can have form (Rupa) and name (Nama)
or name without form; and as we worship Her in
these various aspects we can rise to pure Being,
having neither form nor name.[10]

Just as Sri Ramakrishna incarnated at a time when
Indian culture was being threatened by materialism,
so also Swamiji arrived in the United States at a cusp
in Western culture, when simple religious beliefs were
being undermined by the scientific method, the evo-
lution theory of Charles Darwin, and the Industrial
Revolution. The doctrines of the Church no longer
satisfied the educated classes, who became Swamiji's
audience. To them he spoke his Master's liberal and
liberating message: that God not only exists but can
be realized as a personal fact; that the religions of

10 *Ibid.,* 7.26-7.

the world, including Christianity, are paths leading the sincere to this ultimate goal; that the truths of the Upanishads and methodologies of yoga were not antagonistic to rational inquiry or scientific scrutiny.

Vivekananda's Legacy

As we celebrate Swamiji's 150th birth anniversary, we look up to his legacy. In India he is a national hero, the prophet of the modern Hindu renaissance. We can see practically the transformative influence he has had on his motherland by inspiring generations of his monastic and lay followers to spread education, empower women, uplift the poor, serve the distressed, and distribute spiritual knowledge—all in the name of Sri Ramakrishna, the Avatar of the Age.

But what is his enduring legacy outside of India? As the first Hindu *sannyasin* to preach in America, Swamiji prepared the stage for today's interest in yoga, meditation, ayurveda, kirtan, and the many Hindu-based religious movements that are thriving. But we also see the more subtle effect of Swamiji's work, the effect he has had on the intellectual and spiritual culture of the world. Sri Ramakrishna's realization, "As many faiths, so many paths" was first declared to the West by Swamiji during his opening address at the Parliament of Religions:

> As the different streams having their sources in different places all mingle their water in the sea, so, O Lord, the different paths which men take

through different tendencies, various though they appear, crooked or straight, all lead to Thee.[11]

This once revolutionary idea is now widely accepted, even by many Christians. Although "Vivekananda" is not a household name, his influence has acted as a leavening agent, fundamentally lifting the world-view of millions.

Kali in the West

While in India this universal message has never been separated from the person of Sri Ramakrishna, in the West, we are only beginning to recognize the person behind the principles, the giver of the gift. As Swami Saradananda writes in his masterpiece *Sri Sri Ramakrishna Lilaprasanga*:

> Will people come on their own to accept the Divine Mother's liberal message 'As many faiths, so many paths,' or will they accept it through that person who became the instrument of the Mother and brought that message to the world? The answer to this question, as we understand it, must be determined by the questioner after seeing the result of the full realization of this doctrine either within themselves or in others. Until that realization dawns, silence is the best answer. But if the reader asks what we believe, we say that along with an authentic experience of this liberal

11 *Ibid.,* 1.4.

attitude, one must have a vision of that person whom the Divine Mother, for the first time, sent to embody that doctrine for the good of the world. And one must pour out heartfelt love and respect for him who was free from ego and delusion. The Master will not demand this; no one else will prompt it; love for the Divine Mother will drive one to it spontaneously."[12]

Swamiji arrived in America in 1893. Within seven short years he established a network of societies to promote the teachings of Vedanta. Since then, these have spread to hundreds of centers, ashramas, monasteries, convents, study groups, and home shrines— all dedicated to Sri Ramakrishna.

Swamiji once told Sister Nivedita: "The future, you say, will call Ramakrishna Paramahamsa an Incarnation of Kali? Yes, I think there's no doubt that She worked up the body of Ramakrishna for Her own ends."[13]

When you love someone, you want to love what they love, who they love. Sri Ramakrishna and Mother Kali cannot be separated. Though it has been 120 years since Swamiji first addressed his American sisters and brothers, Mother's work in America is just beginning. She must have a special plan, for She not only sent Vivekananda, but also other direct disciples of Sri Ramakrishna, companions of the avatar, such as Swamis Saradananda, Turiyananda, Abhedananda,

---

12 *Sri Ramakrishna and His Divine Play,* p. 562.
13 *The Master as I Saw Him,* p. 140.

Trigunatitananda, and Nirmalananda—all great saints and knowers of God.

As far as we know, the first traditional worship of Kali in America was performed in the 1940s by Swami Prabhavananda, a disciple of Swami Brahmananda, at Vedanta Society in Hollywood, California. Initially only very close devotees of the society were allowed to attend, for fear of upsetting the puritanical sentiments of their neighbors, or of provoking the cultural biases and prejudices of even some of their own members. But over the years the annual all-night Kali Puja has become more and more popular, a highlight in the devotional lives of both Indian and Western devotees.

Another example of Swamiji's legacy is Kali Mandir in Laguna Beach, California. In 1993 Elizabeth Usha Harding, author of *Kali, the Black Goddess of Dakshineswar*, arranged for a beautiful Kali image to be brought from India, which was ritually awakened by the late Sri Haradhan Chakraborti, the main priest of the Dakshineswar Kali Temple. He named her Sri Ma Dakshineswari Kali and explained that because the image was now 'alive', she needed to be worshiped every day. And Mother arranged for her worship, as devotees who had very little background in the intricacies of India's temple puja standards now found themselves gradually adopting this vastly rich devotional tradition one detail at a time—out of a simple love and desire to please Mother. Haradhanji and his assistant Sri Pranab Ghosal came annually for seventeen years, teaching the devotees Kali puja as practiced in Dakshineswar since the time of Sri

Ramakrishna. There was never an intention to start a temple or establish a monastery. Over time this simple daily worship grew organically and slowly took on the form of a fully-functioning Hindu temple, where devotees, young and old, Western and Indian, householder and renunciant, can pour forth their hearts' yearning to the Great Mystery at the center of existence.

The Path of Love

Sri Ramakrishna's life and teachings point unequivocally towards spiritual freedom. It is not birth, not upbringing, not culture that decides your path. It is yearning. With yearning for the Divine, it does not matter what path you walk; and without yearning, you will not be able to walk any path. Sri Ramakrishna reveals the purest and safest approach to an often misunderstood goddess. There are many ways of worshiping Kali. While many may be authentic, not all are safe. Sri Ramakrishna mastered the sixty-four branches of tantra—many difficult and controversial. But when the time came to train his own disciples, he made the path to God simple and beautiful. He said:

> Call out to Ma with yearning. When you have Her vision, the taste for worldly objects dries up; all attachment to the objects of lust and greed (*kamini-kanchan*) goes away, far into the distance. If you have the feeling that She's your own Mother, it happens immediately. She's not your Godmother. She's your very own Mother!" [14]

---

14   *Sri Sri Ramakrishna Kathamrita*, 1.12.5, trans. by Swami Ambikananda Saraswati.

When Swamiji was in Kashmir, he performed severe austerities. After many nights of intense sadhana at Kshir Bhavani, he had the vision of Mother.

Returning to the houseboat that he and his companions were renting, he raised his hands in benediction and placed the marigolds that he had offered to the goddess on the heads of all of the disciples saying, "No more 'Hari Om!' It is all 'Mother' now! ... I am only a little child!"[15]

Today, more than 150 years after his birth, we are still calculating the tremendous impact this 'little child' has had on the world. Sri Ramakrishna held the key to the Mother's treasure, and Swami Vivekananda, in his brief, blazing life of service, accomplished her work, without a doubt. But Mother's great miracle is that he then left the key for any one of us to find, if we but surrender to her.

"This attitude of regarding God as Mother," Sri Ramakrishna said, "is the last word in sadhana. 'O God, Thou art my Mother and I am Thy child' — this is the last word in spirituality."

---

15 His Eastern and Western Disciples, *The Life of Swami Vivekananda, 2 Vols.*, (Advaita Ashram, Kolkata, 2008), 2.381-2.

2

Kali Puja

The Art of Seeing God

"My Beloved! It is called puja because it destroys the karmas of previous births, ends the cycle of birth and death and grants complete fulfillment."

~ *Kularnava Tantra*

Kali Puja: The Art of Seeing God[1]

Inside, the hush of anticipation is intense. The temple, drenched in predawn murkiness, is full of all types of devotees, diverse souls seeking the same sanctuary at this early hour. Monks sit silently at the foot of the altar, their orange robes almost glowing in the dimness—their fire defies the shadows. No image is to be seen. The large wooden double doors on the altar remain shut. But the light coming from the crack under those doors tells you that something is about to happen. In an instant the hallowed sound of the blowing conch pierces the silence, and as the single note fills every corner of the hall, the doors are opened, light spills everywhere, and a thunderous tumult of bells, gongs and drums announces the glorious awakening of the sleepless, all-powerful Lord. As the eyes of the divine image fall upon you, you fall to your knees, head to the floor, bowing. Then you rise, and the clamor of instruments glides into a natural rhythm as the pujari offers flame, flower, water, perfume and cooling breeze to the living God. The devotees know without a doubt that they have seen God, and that God has seen them. This is *darshan*, the grace and beauty of the Hindu temple: you do not have to be a saint to see God.

This scene is repeated morning after morning in thousands of temples throughout India. Most of the world's major religions teach that God is everywhere and ever-present. Yet these same religions recognize

---

1 This article was co-authored with Swami Ambikananda Saraswati, and first appeared in *Light of Consciousness Magazine*, Winter 2001.

the power and importance of sacred sites; temples, mosques and churches are unlike other buildings. The house of worship holds within it a special manifestation of divinity. Call it an "atmosphere" or a "presence", or whatever you like—it is a quality, immediate and unmistakable, and powerful enough to remind us that the Truth felt within those walls is indeed outside as well. The lens held up to the sunlight will focus the all-pervading rays into a beam powerful enough to burn. If the temple is the lens through which divinity is focused, then within the Hindu temple, the image of the deity is that blazing point of total convergence.

It is surprising that some practitioners of religions who accept the divine presence within the sacred site often have great difficulty in accepting the same presence within the sacred image, and they will usually resort to derisive tones, calling it "idolatry." But to recognize the false, we must have some notion of the true. How does a thing become sacred? What brings about that quality? Why will the devotee trample across one stone presumably to worship another stone? The answer lies within an object's connection to the divine.

> ...There are symbols and symbols, the real ones and the false ones. The mirage has got the appearance of water, but it is a delusive phenomenon which has nothing to do with water; whereas, the wave may be recognized as a true symbol of the ocean, because it rises out of it, is in touch with it, and also gets merged

in it. Like the ocean, it is made of the same substance, water.[2]

The images in Hindu temples are not arbitrary; they are not made up on a whim. These are divine forms, revealed forms, possessing the necessary attributes that separate them from other forms, in the same way that a hundred dollar bill possesses the particular elements that separate it from just another scrap of paper.

While it is true that you do not have to be a saint to see God, there are gradations to darshan. Inside the temple, the saint will not see the deity in the same way as the scoundrel. Just as we all have different physical eyesight, so we all have different spiritual vision. But there is hope, and therein lies the incentive. Although our corporeal vision generally deteriorates as we age, our spiritual vision should only improve. It must improve, and become perfect: that is the goal of *sadhana*, spiritual practice.

If God is everywhere and ever-present, then why is it that we are not continuously stunned in divine rapture? We are not always conscious of the Divine presence. The devotional schools of Hinduism stress the importance of invoking this presence through prayers, chanting and worship.

It is perhaps best to begin a discussion of the elements of traditional worship with the One being worshiped. There are 33 million gods and goddesses in the Hindu pantheon. The label-loving Western mind

---

2 Swami Yatiswarananda, *Meditation and Spiritual Life*, (Ramakrishna Math, Bangalore, 1995), p. 383.

will immediately assume that "Hinduism", itself a label for Sanatana Dharma, the eternal religion of India, is polytheistic—or perhaps henotheistic. Dictionaries and encyclopedias will describe with anemic brevity the "Hindu god of [fill in blank]" or the "goddess of [fill in blank]". Yet if asked, a devout follower of one of those gods or goddesses will say, "I am only worshiping God" (with a capital "G"). As the Rig Veda declares: "Truth is one; sages call it by many names."[3] The same mountain will appear differently when approached from different directions. Theologically speaking, this is a revolutionary thought—even for so-called "sophisticated" modern minds. As a result, we have the concept of the *ishta devata*, or chosen deity. The devotee chooses the face of Truth that is dearest to his or her heart and begins to cultivate a relationship of love, reverence and surrender. We may look upon God as our mother, father, child, friend, or lover. Because the Supreme Being is supremely gracious, we are allowed to approach and to worship that Being in so many beautiful ways. It is this revelation which allows for the incredible richness, variety and complexity within Indian religion.

Before we can truly see everything as divine, we must adopt an attitude of treating everything as divine. But this is not pretense; this is process. The mind and heart must be transformed. One of the easiest ways to purify our heart and mind is to call to the Lord from the depth of our being. God's presence must be invoked and sustained by our heartfelt

---

3 *Rig Veda*, 1.164.46.

prayers and adoration. This is called *puja*. Puja can be as simple as offering your love and aspiration as a flower to the lord of your heart or as intricate as the ritualized worship in public temples.

Each of these approaches carries with it its own unique form of puja. Puja varies according to the deity worshiped, and naturally, the region of practice. Yet there are striking similarities as well, since certain elements of all forms of puja have their collective roots in Tantra. Tantra is the esoteric science of transforming consciousness through dynamic spiritual practices. These elements were absorbed into the Vedic system, eventually finding new expression. Even in modern times diverse traditions continue to influence and enrich one another.

The heart's need for the divine vision is by no means exclusive to India. It is universal. Kali Mandir in Laguna Beach is a traditional temple dedicated to bringing all the beauty and sanctifying power of traditional ritualistic worship to the West. It is a temple of the Divine Mother of the Universe as the loving-fierce form of Goddess Kali. Since its beginning in 1993 Kali Mandir has grown into a beautiful blend of sincere Indian and Western devotees from different lineages, as well as aspirants with no formal affiliations—all attracted by the tangible living presence of the Divine Mother.

Worship is performed daily to the awakened image of Ma Dakshineshwari (the Goddess from Dakshineshwar). The puja performed at Kali Mandir follows the ritualistic tradition of the Dakshineswar Kali Temple, located in Bengal, just outside Kolkata.

This temple is renowned as the place where Sri Ramakrishna Paramahamsa lived, taught, and worshiped the Divine Mother with an awe-inspiring intensity. Dakshineswar has been a beacon for the universality of religion for over a century.

Once a month at Kali Mandir, crowds of Ma's children gather for a special worship held on *amavasya*, the mystic night of the dark moon, an auspicious time for Kali worship. Sincere devotees from far and wide come for this event. They come from all over the state, some driving over four hours to see Her and sing Her names. There are pious Indian families, who come together, sometimes four generations, bowing before Ma simultaneously. Mendicant Hindu monks sit silently, their very presence infusing the atmosphere with sanctity. Young devotees from Los Angeles, pierced, dyed and tattooed, whose pure-hearted sincerity will bring tears to your eyes, sit together waiting with anticipation. Old, young, spiritual geniuses and the slightly crazy—they all find their way to Mother's feet. A glimpse of the devotees can change your life as quickly and thoroughly as a glimpse of the Mother.

The puja is performed by a pujari, someone who is trained in the technical nuances of traditional ritual. The pujari's main function is to call forth Divinity, to make the Divine Presence felt. To do this he or she must first awaken the Divinity within through a sequence of purifying acts, each one operating on increasingly subtler levels.

With our actions, mind and speech, we have no other goal than You, Who by dwelling within, witnesses all beings, O Supreme Goddess.

This prayer, recited at the end of the puja, beautifully conveys the essence of devotional worship. The act of puja is a conscious redirecting of our mind and the senses toward the ever-present Divinity. Our speech becomes purified through the recitation of the sacred mantras used in puja; our actions become purified through the use of hand gestures (*mudra*), breath control (*pranayama*), and the physical offering of gifts to the Divine. Our thoughts become purified through the various meditations and visualizations occurring throughout the worship. Redirection, purification, and transformation: this is the process by which the Divine is awakened.

Dusk has settled. The altar is sparkling clean and exquisitely decorated. Garlands of marigolds adorn the images, while trays piled with flowers await offering. The lamps and incense are lit. The pujari comes before the altar, bows, and sits down to meditate for a short time before starting. The outgoing mind must now withdraw and patiently focus on the inner world.

As if being cued, everyone present settles down and begins to withdraw. It is now so quiet you could hear a feather drop. Once in a while we encounter moments so peaceful, they seem like the soft pause between the breaths of life itself. This is one of them. Serene silence, the flickering of oil lamps, and the gentle curling of fragrant incense: God is waiting.

Slowly the pujari puts his hands together and begins to pray:

May auspiciousness come from our Divine Guru. May auspiciousness come from our Divine Mother. May auspiciousness come from devotees of the Lord. May auspiciousness come from all the worlds.

This prayer helps to remind us that devotion is a gift. Remembering this helps develop the humility necessary for spiritual advancement. It is by the grace of our teachers, the devotees, and the Divine Mother Herself that we are blessed with the privilege and opportunity to worship Her. The pujari, on behalf of the assembled devotees, therefore invokes their blessings before beginning the puja.

All the mantras used in puja are spoken in Sanskrit. Each mantra is a sacred formula, divine consciousness as sound vibrations. In linguistics there is the concept of the speech act. For example, the speaking of a marriage vow is itself the act of becoming married. When spoken with a focused will, words have a tremendous power. Considering that ordinary words possess the power to win or break hearts, topple governments, and transform civilizations, what can be said of the power of sanctified speech?

The pujari then begins the first stage of purification. Three times, he pours a spoonful of water in his right palm, infuses it with the name of Vishnu, and sips. The scriptures stress the importance of sipping water charged with mantras (*acamana*), for purification at the beginning of any religious act. The worshiper feels that this consecrated water, like the Ganges, is flowing from the holy feet of the Lord.

Water is a central element in puja. This water receives its purifying power through mantra. In front of the pujari is the copper vessel and offering spoon that represents the womb of the Divine Mother. The pujari fills this vessel with water and begins to show a series of mudras. His hands hover and glide, like birds, over this water, as if speaking fluently in some beautiful sign language. The sacred rivers (Ganga, Yamuna, Godavari, Saraswati, Narmada, Sindhu, and Kaveri), all of them personified Goddesses, are invoked into this water which will now serve as an important purifying agent throughout the rest of the puja.

Puja contains syntax unique unto itself, employing sacred conventions to express spiritual intentions. The mudra is an example of one such convention. Mudras are hand gestures that, like mantras, embody certain energies. The hands naturally express emotions and ideas: we make fists when angry, throw up our hands when frightened or disgusted, wave, point, etc. Similarly, certain hand gestures can express spiritual ideas. Mudras also help concentrate the mind by unifying body, mind and vital force (*prana*).

Shifting into a position almost resembling the Catholic genuflection, the pujari recites the *sankalpa*, the formal declaration of pure intent. This keeps us mindful of our purpose in performing the ritual. It is extremely dangerous to worship God with selfish motives.

Sri Ramakrishna would pray, "Oh Mother! I do not crave bodily comforts. I do not want name and fame. I do not seek the eight occult powers. I only want pure love for Thy Lotus Feet!"

The pujari now draws a yantra with water under his seat, and offers it flowers, honoring and sanctifying Mother Earth. Then the altar and articles of worship are subtly purified with sprinkling of water and chanting of mantras. The system of puja is a tradition handed down from guru to disciple. The pujari invokes his lineage of gurus (*sampradaya*), connecting himself with this unbroken chain of grace and placing himself at a specific point within sacred time. The pujari next places himself at a specific point within sacred space. Through the sanctity of the worship itself, the place of worship becomes the holy yantra or realm of the Goddess. This yantra has ten main entrance points: the eight cardinal directions, and above and below. It is through these that energy can enter and leave the yantra. The pujari moves his hand around his head, snapping his fingers while uttering the protective mantra "*phat*", sealing these points, in order to contain the divine energies invoked during the worship.

Pouring water from the palm of his hand around himself, the pujari imagines being protected by a ring of fire. As our concentration deepens and our hearts begin to open up, we become sensitive to negative energies and astral entities. This process creates a safe environment for performing the internal practices that follow.

As these opening rituals continue, one of the many expert musicians begins to sing to the accompaniment of harmonium, drums and hand cymbals.

Some devotees continue to meditate throughout the kirtan. This call-and-response devotional chanting is a great way to personally experience the transformative power and beauty of God's many holy names.

Meanwhile the pujari begins performing *pranayama*. *Prana* refers to the vital force that animates our body and mind, and manifests outwardly as our breath. *Ayama* means control and expansion. Pranayama is the practice through which this vital air is consciously controlled or directed. While mentally chanting a mantra, the breath is inhaled, held and exhaled through alternating nostrils in a series of sequential durations. This quiets the mind and purifies the 72,000 subtle nerves in the body, allowing the free flow of prana and the awakening of *kundalini shakti*, the Divine Mother as the power of consciousness residing in the body.

As only diamond can cut diamond, the Tantric scriptures declare that "Divinity alone can worship Divinity." The body and mind need to be divinized. All the purification that has taken place so far goes to support the following practice, one of the most crucial in puja, known as *bhutashuddhi*. Consciousness, divine by nature, has no material form or shape, but rather takes on the qualities of its container. Therefore the whole process of bhutashuddhi is to purify the container, the body and mind. According to Tantra, this body and mind are composed of five gross elements (earth, water, fire, air, ether), and three subtle elements (mind, intelligence, ego). In bhutashuddhi, all of these principles undergo total purification.

With the body and mind now purified, the Divine Mother can be invoked within the heart through the appropriate mantras and mudras. The pujari now creates a proper spiritual body for Her, in place of his own. The *Maha-Lakshmyashtakam* states, "The form of the Goddess consists only of mantra (*mantra murti sada devi*)." According to Tantric philosophy, creation begins with vibration. The supreme vibration is the universal sound Om, which then differentiates Itself into the fifty unique sounds of the Sanskrit alphabet. These sound-letters join to create the world of name and form. Each letter is recognized as a *matrika*, or mother-goddess. Through the process of *nyasa*, each matrika is placed and worshiped within the pujari's body.

The excitement continues to build as the pujari begins the traditional preliminary worship. The guru is honored first, since the guru is the human channel of divine grace. Next Lord Ganesha, the elephant-headed son of Shiva and Parvati, is worshiped as the remover of our material and spiritual obstacles. Then the five Vedic deities (Shiva, Vishnu, Surya, Durga, and Agni) are honored, connecting us with ancient tradition. As perfume, flower, incense, light, and sweets are offered, the music of the kirtan becomes intoxicating. The drums and cymbals beat faster, and the singing falls into harmony with the pujari's chanting.

Reciting a verse (*dhyana-mantra*) that describes the vision of Mother Kali seen by the sages, the pujari places a flower on his head and mentally worships the Goddess within his heart. He now prepares for the invocation of the all-pervading Mother into the image. This is the moment of *prana pratishtana*, when God is humbly asked to come, sit, and face the assembled devotees. These mantras and mudras are some of the most powerful ones used in the puja, and it is not difficult to perceive the manifestation taking place. That transcendent Reality, in the form of the Goddess, now stands before us to receive our worship.

This is the magic moment. She is here! The devotees feel Her presence. The Subtle One has become obvious. The Absolute Existence, Knowledge and Bliss, invoked within the pujari's heart and projected into the holy image can be seen and experienced. The devotees, all different and unique, offer their love, prayers, concerns, complaints and aspirations to their Mother. Does She listen? Is it only imagination? The full hearts and shining faces of Her devotees give the answer.

The pujari raises his hands before the Divine Mother, beckoning Her to sit. He offers Her welcome, washes Her feet, and gives Her water and sweet milk to drink. He bathes Her, clothes Her, gives Her bangles and other ornaments, perfume, hibiscus (Ma's favorite flower), garlands, incense and light. These external offerings are the symbolic tokens of our inner love, devotion and respect. We want relationship. We want to see God.

Assistants clear space on the altar, making room for Mother's meal. Trays and trays of cooked foods, sweets, fruits, and refreshing spices are brought and laid before Her. The mood suddenly changes and the devotees sing soulful songs while their dear Mother enjoys Her meal. When She is finished, the trays of food are taken back to the kitchen. This food having been partaken by God is now *prasad* and is considered purified and blessed. The devotees will feast on Her mercy after the puja.

The pujari stands and blows the conch. All rise for the concluding arati. The air is now electric. Every voice in the temple is glorifying the Divine Mother, chanting *Jai Ma Jai Ma Jai Ma Jai Ma*! (Victory to the Mother!), while every pair of hands, every bell, drum, and cymbal, claps and clangs in unison. The pujari offers a ghee lamp with five wicks, gently circling it around Her image. Then he offers a spoon of burning camphor, water from a bathing conch, cloth, flower, and fan. The conch is blown again three times, declaring spiritual victory, as all bow to Ma. Symbolically, the elements of the material universe are being offered back into their Source. But for the devotees present, this is simply the natural way to adore the Mother—the art of seeing God.

3

Kirtan

Singing the Divine Name

"Chant the Name of the Lord and His glories
unceasingly that the mirror of the heart
may be wiped clean."

~ Sri Chaitanya, *Shashtikam*

Kirtan: Singing the Divine Name[1]

God in Seed Form

My guru, Swami Vishnudevananda Saraswati of Allahabad, explained the dynamics of chanting in this way. He told me that if you sow a thought, you reap a deed because thought precedes action. If you sow a deed, you reap a habit because deeds repeated become habit. If you sow a habit, you reap a character because the sum total of our habits is our character. If you sow a character, you reap a destiny because our character determines whom we become. I remember his voice very clearly saying, "Thought is all important. Think only divine thoughts. God is the highest thought."

All spiritual practices are designed to help us focus on God. We are doing puja, singing kirtan, having satsang, reciting shlokas, meditating on mantras—all to fill our mind with divine thoughts. If we sow God-thoughts then our actions become spiritual, our habits become pure and our character becomes saintly. A saint thinks only of God—there is no second thought. The plant has blossomed. We see in such a person so much devotion, so much love. Divine character is our destiny. Guruji always told me that character is everything.

Sowing implies a seed. A seed contains within it the potentiality of the entire tree. What is the seed form of God? The name of God is such a seed. For me

---

1 Transcript of a talk given at Kali Mandir, originally published in *Namarupa* magazine, Winter 2004.

the single most important revelation in spiritual life is that the name of God is God. The great Himalayan yogi Swami Sivananda Saraswati of Rishikesh said, "All divine potencies, all powers, all divine qualities are hidden in God's name."

If we plant this seed deep within our consciousness, it will grow and transform us. If it is planted properly in fertile soil, guarded properly and weeded, it will blossom very quickly.

The question then becomes, "How do we bring the holy name deep into our consciousness?" Our problem is that our minds have become habituated to external thinking. This is because the function of the senses is to bring us information from the outside world. Out of habit, our minds are attached to the outgoing senses and therefore go outward as well. In Pantanjali's yoga system after restraints (*yama*), observances (*niyama*), posture (*asana*), and breath control (*pranayama*) comes the very difficult requirement of the withdrawal of the mind from the outside world of the senses (*pratyahara*). We have to reel this mind in somehow or other. Otherwise concentration (*dharana*), meditation (*dhyana*) and absorption (*samadhi*) are not possible. But the mind is very tricky. The mind does not want to come in. The senses are very turbulent and the mind is completely identified with them. What to do?

The Path for this Dark Age

It is said in the Puranic literature that kirtan is the easiest method for God-realization in the Kali Yuga, the present dark age. This was the central message of Sri Chaitanya Mahaprabhu more than five hundred years ago as well as an important teaching of Sri Ramakrishna Paramahamsa in more recent times. If we are honest and humble, we can see that our position has become almost hopeless. The whole atmosphere is against us. We have no good training. Even if we had loving wonderful parents, did they train us how to control the mind, to internalize it, to detach it from the senses, and to focus on inner spiritual realities? Our modern culture is pushing us to become selfish and materialistic. But in this, our darkest hour, the holy names of God have descended as a golden umbrella during a dark rain.

How does kirtan help our externalized mind become internalized? Our senses are our weak points. If something is nice looking in front of us, how would we desire not to look at it? We have to look at it. If something is beautiful sounding, how could we desire not to listen to it? But we can use our weakness to our advantage by connecting our senses with God. We must stamp God on everything. Then everywhere our mind and senses go, we will find only God.

"Music tames the wild beast." The wild beast is our own mind attached to the outgoing senses. Everybody is attracted to beautiful music. If that beautiful music is based upon God's name and glories, our mind can be internalized, because God is the deepest reality of our being. Even though we are listening externally, what we are hearing is a reflection of the inner reality.

We generally listen to music and sing to entertain ourselves. Hence, there is the danger of using the holy name and kirtan as entertainment. The holy name is God Himself, the Goddess Herself, Brahman Itself—not entertainment. Entertainment is something that happens on the surface level of consciousness. Eventually we have to go beyond kirtan as entertainment. A seed only works if it is planted *in* the ground.

Inner Attitude During Kirtan

The principles for bringing the holy name deep into our consciousness in kirtan, although mostly unknown in the Western world, are revealed by the devotional scriptures and the nada-yogis who understand the transforming power of holy sound.

We get excited about chanting, but often do not understand what our inner attitude should be. Swami Sivananda writes:

> When you sing Hari's name, feel that the Lord is seated in your heart, that every name of the Lord is filled with divine potencies, that the old vicious *samskaras* (thought and behavior patterns) and *vasanas* (mental waves) are burnt by the power of the Name, that the mind is filled with purity, that passion and inertia are completely destroyed and that the veil of ignorance is torn down. Meditate on His form and attributes also. Then only will you get maximum benefit from kirtan.[2]

Kirtan is our calling out to God.

---

2 Swami Sivananda, *Bhakti and Sankirtan*, Divine Life Society (Rishikesh, 1984), p. 104.

In the bhakti-yoga tradition of the *Bhagavat-Purana* it is mentioned that there are nine primary practices or forms of devotion. They are hearing (*shravanam*), chanting (*kirtanam*), remembering (*smaranam*), offering prayers (*vandhanam*), serving the Lord's feet (*pada-sevanam*), becoming a servant (*dasanam*), worship (*pujana*), befriending (*sakhi-jana*), and self-surrender (*atma-nivedana*). All this starts with hearing, chanting, and remembering. These three are the secret of kirtan.

The Mala in Kirtan

The most popular form of kirtan is based upon call and response. One person leads the chant and we listen. Then we repeat the chant and the leader listens. When we respond we should chant as sweetly and as devotionally as we can. And in our chanting we should also be listening. We should learn to hear the sincerity in our chanting. This will adjust our inner attitude. The whole time we must try to remember God, who mercifully appears in the form of the holy name. The purpose is God-remembrance.

Just as we often use a *mala* or rosary when chanting *japa*, we need a mala in kirtan as well. In japa we chant a mantra and go on to the next bead, chant a mantra and go on to the next bead, chant a mantra, etc. When we are finished with one, the next one comes automatically. The mala keeps the mantra rotating in consciousness and stabilizes our mind during meditation. In kirtan it is the tune and the rhythm that push the mantra forward and keeps the mind focused. They are the next bead. It is important that kirtan singers and musicians remember this. In japa you create your own rhythm, bead after bead, breath after breath.

Swami Sivananda says, "There must be perfect harmony and concord, one tune (*svara*), one rhythm (*tala*), when *sankirtan* is conducted. Then only there will be joy and elevation of the mind."[3]

The Energetic Mystery

When you sing kirtan or perform an elaborate ritual, everywhere the mind goes it will find the holy name. The mind gets focused. All of our scattered thoughts become one thought—one *vritti*. A vritti is a wave or ripple in the mind, any mental modification. The yogis describe it in this way. These thoughts united become a big wave in consciousness which energetically rises up the spine, touching the thousand-petaled lotus at the top of the head. The top of the head is full of nectar which, when touched by this wave, falls in a shower of spiritual magnetism. During a very good kirtan you can sometime feel a downward flow of subtle energy. This is the nectar (*amrita*) that is falling. It is a very internal yogic experience. We must try to get our mind, emotions, sentiments, and energies focused in one direction. When they move in one direction—how much power! In a really good kirtan, everyone is stunned, amazed. Just jumping around with excitement will often get us agitated externally. But the name will not go very

---

3 *Ibid.*, p. 89

deep. There is a difference between agitated kirtan and kirtan that takes us beyond our body and mind. "Spiritual freedom" means freedom *from* the senses, not *of* the senses.

A Strong Warning

The holy name is not a product to be sold and kirtan is not a performance or concert. Kirtan is worship, not entertainment. When kirtan becomes a career, then pleasing the crowd can become more important than meditation on the holy name. As a result, the focus is drifting away from the traditional methods of using sacred sound to invoke God's purifying presence. Some argue that this is simply an adjustment of the ancient traditions of kirtan to suit the Western modern mind. But we must remember that it is our mental conditioning that keeps us in bondage. Spiritual practice is meant to remove our ignorance and conditioning, not reinforce them. It is easy to delude ourselves into thinking we are advancing spiritually. The art and practice of kirtan must be protected. Kirtan leaders have a great responsibility and must become serious spiritual practitioners.

Along with kirtan, the sages teach that we must seek the company and advice of saints and elders, study the scriptures deeply, chant japa and meditate regularly, engage in deep self-inquiry, consciously develop virtues, struggle to eradicate vices and practice the yogic restraints (*yamas*) and observances (*niyamas*). These are the foundations of a true spiritual life. If we build a building without a foundation then we are really building an accident.

According to the bhakti-yoga traditions, the religion of the age (*yuga-dharma*) is the chanting of God's names. Chaitanya Mahaprabhu, Sri Ramakrishna, Anandamayi Ma, Neem Karoli Baba, Swami Ramdas and other great saints of this age have repeatedly said this. It is important to know how it works and for that we need valuable guidance from traditional sources. In order to have something stable, you need at least three legs. These are *guru*, *sadhu* and *shastra*. Gurus are our spiritual teachers and elders. Sadhus are monks, nuns, advanced devotees and other holy people. Shastras are the sacred scriptures and oral traditions. If we base our spiritual life upon these three then we are safe and can progress carefully and surely. Otherwise we may find that at the end of our life we have gotten nowhere—that we were given everything but gained nothing. To me, this is the most frightening of possibilities.

The privilege of knowing, meditating upon, singing, and serving the divine name is God's merciful gift to us. May the divine seed of the holy name grow and flourish, purifying our hearts, and may we enjoy the harvest of pure devotion.

4

Japa Yoga

"The Divine Name is the antidote for all of our misery, sorrow, depravity and malignity. Soak your mind with the Lord's Name. Merge yourself in the inner light and sound. That is the Divine Ground."

~ *Swami Vishnudevananda Saraswati*

Japa Yoga

Mantra Meditation

The goal of yoga and meditation is the purification of our consciousness leading to absorption in God. We have much in our hearts and minds that obscures rather than reveals sacred reality. Our natural loving sentiments towards God are distorted, preventing us from experiencing the all-blissful Self. Thought determines the quality of our lives. We sow a thought and reap an action. We sow an action and reap a habit. We sow a habit and reap a character. We sow a character and reap a destiny. Thought precedes and leads to action. Action repeated becomes established as habit. The sum total of our habits is our character. Our character determines the end result of our lives.

Thought is all-important. We have created our present life and experiences by our past thoughts and actions, and we are creating our future life and experiences by our present thoughts and actions. Knowing this, we can transform our life and consciousness by deliberately filling our mind with the highest, most positive thought. This thought is God. For sadhana to be effective we must plant God in seed form. A seed contains the entire tree in potential form. All that we know of the tree and all that remains unknown about the tree is present in its seed. If we plant a seed in good soil and care for it carefully, then the tree will grow in all its glory. God's name is the infinite God in seed-form. This God-seed is called mantra. By the sowing of this God-seed we spiritualize our thoughts. Spiritual thoughts give rise to spiritual actions. Spiritual actions develop a spiritual character. A spiritual character leads to ultimate absorption in God. Repeating God's name is the easiest and surest method to effect this divine transformation. This process is known as *japa yoga*. Japa yoga is the conscious attempt to divinize our consciousness by repeatedly planting divine thoughts deeper and deeper into our minds.

The sages declare that God's name is different than other names. God being absolute, His/Her name is also absolute. God's name is God. All divine powers are contained in the holy name. The Lord and His name are the same! This is a revolutionary thought! It seems too simple. We want our spiritual life to be more dramatic and complicated than simple repetition of a holy mantra. Be careful not to throw away this great treasure because of its seeming simplicity.

Mantras have traditionally been handed down through the ages from guru to disciple and it is best to receive them through disciplic succession (*guru-parampara*). The guru parampara is the river of grace in our lives. Through the process of initiation the guru mystically plants the mantra deep into the consciousness of the disciple. By sincerely repeating the mantra and following the guru's instructions concerning the lifestyle and related practices that support its transforming influence, steady and sure progress can be made, and the obstacles that arise during practice can be overcome or avoided. The guru acts as a divine matchmaker, connecting the aspirant and the Lord through the medium of mantra.

Sri Ramakrishna taught that absolute existence, knowledge and bliss (*sat-chit-ananda*) is the only guru. God is the guru. God as teacher is called guru. This does not mean that our human teacher is God, rather our teacher is an instrument for God, as the guru-principle (*guru-tattva*), to flow to us. The human guru is our channel of grace. The person you accept initiation from should know the scriptures, be well established upon the spiritual path, be able to answer your spiritual questions, have no selfish agenda for teaching you, and be sincerely following and properly initiated in a traditional lineage. If you find such a person and feel drawn to him or her you can request initiation. Upon initiation, he or she becomes your initiating guru (*diksha-guru*). Guru-tattva can also act through other pure souls to give us guidance, teachings and blessings. These teachers are known as instructing guru (*shiksha-guru*) and auxiliary guru (*upa-guru*). Our gurus should always be treated with respect and appreciation. The bond between guru and disciple is sacred and must never be taken for granted.

If you have not yet found your guru, do not be discouraged. You should start by repeating the name of God that appeals to you most. All that is needed is sincerity and devotion—a yearning for God-experience.

The form of God you love most and are most attracted to is known as the *ishta-devata*. God is infinite and has infinite names and forms. Sometimes the guru reveals the ishta devata, but you will usually know within your heart which divine form is your own. Ultimately God chooses you. Whomever the ishta devata, always remember that there is only one God and try to see this God in all divine manifestations. Each ishta devata has corresponding mantras that sonically embody the deity. The guru chooses which mantra is best suited for the disciple's practice. It is not advisable to whimsically change your chosen deity or mantra. There are many paths to God, but one must walk primarily on only one of them.

Preliminary Instruction in Japa Sadhana

What follows is the traditional method of planting God's name deep into consciousness known as japa yoga or mantra yoga. Yogic adepts and devotees throughout the ages have experimented with different methods of meditation on the Lord's names, and we should try to benefit from their experience. If you start by developing good habits in meditation, your progress will be steady and permanent.

If possible your morning sadhana should begin before sunrise. This is the holy *brahma-muhurta*, when spiritual practice is most effective. The environment is quiet and pure at this time. Whether or not you wake up for brahma muhurta, start the day with God by sitting for meditation first thing in the morning. Your evening meditation should be at sunset or as close to sunset as possible. If for some reason you cannot sit at this auspicious time, be sure to sit sometime before going to bed. At the junctures of the day (sunrise, noon, sunset and midnight) our life energies (*prana*) flow evenly, allowing deeper concentration of mind. By meditating during the early morning and evening, we also benefit from the holy vibrations of the sages, earth, elements, planets and divine beings released at this time. Always take a bath before your morning meditation, and if possible, before your evening sitting as well.

After bathing, dress in clean clothes used only for spiritual practice. This cloth will become infused with the vibration of your sadhana, and through mental and physical association your mind will become meditative simply by wearing such cloth. Special clothes for meditation are helpful but not absolutely necessary. It is best if you can have a separate room or corner of a room where you can daily practice meditation and worship. Mantras have much power and the place where they are chanted becomes charged with spiritual vibrations. By sitting in the same place everyday for your practice, you can benefit from this holy atmosphere. Your meditation room or corner should be arranged like a temple by establishing a shrine where God is invited to stay and be worshiped. We must make God the center of our life. Your altar should minimally have a picture, painting or image of your ishta devata and a picture of your guru. You can also have any other pictures or images of deities and saints that inspire you or with whom you have a spiritual connection. Before starting your meditation, bow to your guru and ishta devata, and light an oil lamp or candle and some incense. This purifies the atmosphere and helps focus the mind on God.

Sit in a meditation pose on your personal meditation seat (*asana*). This asana should be made of natural fibers such as cotton, silk, fine wool or kusha grass, and only be used for spiritual practice. Your asana will prevent the dispersion of the energies invoked during sadhana and will become highly magnetized with spiritual vibrations. No one else should use your asana.

We should gradually attain the ability to sit in one posture for a long time (*asana-jaya*). The lotus posture (*padmasana*) is the ideal position for meditation because the back, head and neck are naturally in a straight line, allowing the free flow of blood, prana and kundalini shakti. This posture also keeps you awake and makes the body feel firm. The natural locks (*bandas*) that are part of this posture also keep your energies from flowing outward, allowing for deeper inward concentration. Although you should sit upright, all your muscles should be relaxed and free from strain. If the lotus posture is not possible, you can sit in any comfortable upright position. Try to sit in one posture for as long as you can during meditation. If your legs get numb or your back starts hurting, then shift your position for a while and go back to your original posture as soon as you can. A small pillow under the hips can help.

Recite some elevating prayers invoking the blessings of Ganesha, your gurus and ishta devata. This uplifts and concentrates the mind. Always remember that devotion, meditative aspiration and spiritual realization come to us through grace alone.

Take three to ten deep, even and silent breaths mentally chanting "Om". Pranayama balances the energies of the body and calms the mind. Pranayama also destroys sins, purifies the astral body's 72,000 subtle nerves, awakens kundalini shakti and improves mental and physical health. Other forms of pran-ayama, such as alternate nostril breathing, should be learned only from a qualified teacher.

Sit quietly, relaxing your body and mind. If you spend a few moments quietly watching the mind, it will soon turn to you for direction. Visualize your guru seated in lotus-posture upon a twelve-petaled lotus resting upon the top of your head. Feel your mantra at the root of the tongue. Visualize your ishta devata shining within the lotus of your heart. Now visualize your guru merging into the mantra, and the mantra into the ishta devata in the heart. The inner light (*antar-jyoti*) is the Soul of your soul. The man-tra, ishta devata, guru, and antar jyoti are different aspects of the same reality upon which you meditate.

Now begin to mentally repeat your mantra, keep-ing count on your rosary (*japa-mala*) or on your fin-gers. Repeat at least one round of 108 mantras in this way. This should be your minimum for your morn-ing and evening meditations. Increase the number of malas you chant as you progress in your practice. You can also chant without counting by fixing a certain time period of practice.

Japa Mala

The mala should be made of holy beads such as *tulsi*, *rudraksha* or *spatik*. Tulsi beads are carved from the wood of Indian sacred basil and are only used for chanting the names of Vishnu and His incarnations.

Rudraksha beads are the seeds from a holy tree sacred to Lord Shiva and are used when chanting mantras to Shiva or forms of the Goddess. Spatik beads are made from Himalayan quartz crystal and are used for goddess (*shakti*) mantras alone. A japa mala helps stabilize the mind, keeps the mantra rotating in consciousness and keeps you focused. To use a japa mala, start by holding the first bead next to the *meru* with the thumb and middle finger of your right hand. The meru is the main bead, often larger with tassel. Repeat the mantra and move on to the next bead, and so on. Never cross over or chant on the meru bead. When you finish the mala and wish to continue, then turn the mala around and start again making the last bead your first one. The japa mala becomes spiritually magnetized and should be treated with reverence. Your japa mala should not be worn while passing stool or urine and should not touch your feet or the floor. Others should not touch it unnecessarily.

Akshara-Shuddhi

Purity of letters (*akshara-shuddhi*) is very important. When repeating mantra, mentally pronounce each syllable correctly and distinctly. Your attention should be on the sacred sounds of the mantra and their meaning. Loving adoration of the ishta devata is the goal. Over time, the mantra will move from the surface levels of the mind into deeper and deeper levels of consciousness. Feel that the sound of the mantra is divinity itself and is healing, transforming and illuminating your mind and heart. Strive to be conscious of your ishta devata shining within the heart and feel the loving presence of God showering you with blessings as you repeat the beautiful and sanctifying divine name. Whenever the mind wanders from the mantra, instead of trying to fight the distractions, simply bring your mind back to the sound and meaning of the mantra. Closing the eyes during meditation helps internalize the mind by shutting out external distractions and decreasing brain wave activity. You may, from time to time, open your eyes and gaze upon your ishta devata and guru. This is especially helpful when concentration wavers.

Varieties of Japa

Mental japa is considered the most effective form of mantra meditation, but the mind likes variety. The mantra can also be chanted out loud or in a whisper. This is helpful when the mind is very restless or overcome with sleep, but do this only when there is no one near enough to hear you. Never reveal your mantra to anyone. It is between you, your guru and God.

Keep Mood Intact

Before getting up from your meditation, you can recite some prayers and spend some time singing the Lord's names or simply praying in the language of the heart. As you bow and leave your meditation seat, it is important to keep the mantra going and the spiritual vibrations intact. The mantra should not be limited to formal meditation sessions. The simple rule of spiritual life is "always repeat your mantra". This is all important. The mantra must become second nature. Start repeating your mantra upon awaking in the morning and continue to chant while falling asleep at night. As soon as you realize that you have stopped chanting, simply start again. The mantra will soon become the underlying reality of your life. Then God will become the underlying reality of your life.

Never forget that the real purpose of this human life is the realization of God. This can be gloriously attained through the constant invocation of God's holy names, chanting the mantra with every breath, living in the name. Please start now. God's name is infallible. May the compassionate Lord bless you with lifelong devotion to His holy names.

5

Moment by Moment
Worship

"O Lord Shiva, You are indeed that inexpressible truth
which yogis realize within through concentrating
their minds on the Self and controlling their breath
according to the directions given in the scriptures,
realizing which they experience thrills of rapture and
shed profuse tears of ecstasy. Swimming in a pool of
nectar they revel in inner bliss."

~ *Shiva Mahimna Stotram of Pushpadanta*

Moment by Moment Worship

The following beautiful mantra is part of the internal worship (*manasa-puja*) given in the Tantric scriptures. It describes the flower offerings made of inner feeling in the worship of Shiva (*bhaava-push-paih sampuujayet shivam*).

अहिंसा परमं पुष्पम्
पुष्पमिन्द्रियनिग्रः
दयापुष्पं क्षमापुष्पं
ज्ञानपुष्पं च पञ्चमम् ॥

ahiṁsā paramaṁ puṣpam
puṣpam-indriyanigraḥ
dayā-puṣpaṁ kṣamā-puṣpaṁ
jñāna-puṣpaṁ ca pañcamam

The supreme flower of non-violence,
the flowers of control of the senses,
the flower of compassion,
the flower of forgiveness,
and the flower of wisdom
—these are the five flowers.

Ahimsa paramam pushpam

Non-violence (*ahimsa*) is living high ideals in daily life. The One we love exists in all beings. Every time we choose the option that causes the least possible harm and suffering to others, this is choosing love, dignity and respect. Our conscious choices in diet, clothes, words and actions become the supreme flowers (*paramam pushpam*) of selfless love in our worship of Shiva, and Shiva reciprocates with this act of love by keeping our karma, conscience and lifestyle pure.

Pushpam indriya-nigraha

Indriya refers to the five senses. Indriya also means controller. We are usually controlled by our senses instead of using them as instruments given by God for living a life of service, joy and transcendence. *Indriya-nigrah* is gaining control of the controllers. This is done be following pure precepts that represent pathways for purifying our relationship with our bodies, other people and the world we live in. There is no pleasure in seeking pleasure. Only suffering and degradation come from losing our independence to uncontrolled senses. Real joy comes from simple, loving and dharmic relationships within a life of God-communion.

Daya-pushpam

Compassion (*daya*) is a quality of the soul. Every act of mercy, charity, duty and kindness reveals this divine quality. By living simply, much energy, time and wealth are freed for service of Shiva living in the hearts of all.

Kshama pushpam

Forgiving someone who has hurt us, especially if humbly requested by them, unties a knot in the heart. This also awakens compassion, as we learn to recognize how the struggles of others inform their bad decisions and selfish, hurtful or thoughtless behavior. Forgiving others and ourselves does not mean lowering our ideals, standards or expectations, but rather understanding the obstacles we all face as we struggle to grow and mature. Every act of forgiveness, or of asking others to forgive us, is a manifestation of the innate humility of the soul before God.

Jnana pushpam

Wisdom (*jnana*) is the fruit of spiritual living. It is distinct from the knowledge and expertise that comes through education and training. Wisdom does not come from outside. Wisdom is an inherent quality of the soul. It is not learned. It manifests. In the sadhu tradition we term it *puran-ved*, that ancient knowledge that we have forgotten over many lives of selfish striving. Contemplation of sacred texts, company of devotees, living simply and close to the rhythms of nature, and daily spiritual practice help us remember the reality that has always been there, just behind our fluctuating thoughts. Wisdom manifests as clear understanding, purified intuition and direct revelation. Wisdom is Shiva worshiping Himself.

Cha panchamam

Offering these five flowers is a moment-to-moment sacrifice of selfishness and separateness, the tools of the ego. This is a recognition of the One who pervades everything and everyone, including ourselves, and who manifests *as* everything and everyone, including ourselves. In order to sustain this internal offering, it is also important to chant the divine mantra in sadhana morning and evening, to invoke and honor the divine at home through daily puja and prayers, and to regularly worship at temples surcharged with divine presence. By the grace of Lord Shiva every act and every thought becomes a loving offering. God then is our center, our foundation, our reality and our destination.

6

Bhagavatam Meditations

"Bhakti–Yoga is a real, genuine search after the Lord,
a search beginning, continuing, and ending in love.
One single moment of the madness of extreme love
to God brings us eternal freedom."

~ *Swami Vivekananda*

Bhagavatam Meditations

Our Real Master

श्रियः पतिर् यज्ञपतिः प्रजापतिर्
धियां पतिर् लोकपतिर् धरापतिः ।
पतिर् गतिश् चान्धकवृष्णिसात्वतां
प्रसीदताम् मे भगवान् सतां पतिः ॥

śriyaḥ patir yajña-patiḥ prajā-patir
dhiyāṁ patir loka-patir dharā-patiḥ
patir gatiś cāndhaka-vṛṣṇi-sātvatāṁ
prasīdatām me bhagavān satāṁ patiḥ

Lord of Sri, master of sacrifice, Lord of creators, controller of intelligence, master of the worlds, Lord of the earth, guide and destination of the Yadu kings such as Andhaka and Vrishni—please be merciful to me, O Blessed Lord, master of the devotees.

~ *Srimad Bhagavat Mahapurana* 2:4:20

This prayer recognizes the nature of God as the master (*pati*) of everything. God is called the Lord of Sri (*shriya pati*). Opulence, glory, fame, wealth, luck and success all taken together are denoted by the word Sri, an appellation of Goddess Lakshmi, the consort of Lord Vishnu. In our foolishness, we are trying to become lords of Sri, but this is never possible. Her nature is fickle, she comes and goes. Instead we are encouraged to worship her lord, for where God is, all auspicious qualities are present automatically. The term *yajna-pati* means that God is the master and goal of all religious sacrifices. Often worship, vows, austerities, and charity are performed to generate merit or good karma leading to fame, pleasure, progeny and wealth in this world, and residence in heaven after death. It is the Lord who grants these rewards. But when all acts are performed only to please God and purify our consciousness, then they generate devotion to God, the ultimate goal of sacrifice. God is *praja-pati*, the chief progenitor, the "uncaused cause" of all life. He is called *dhiyam-pati*, the director of our mental faculties. Consciousness is divine and animates our inner instruments, such as mind, intellect and ego-sense, but the ego seems to be in control. By developing our intuition and the mood of self-surrender, we make God the direct master of our mind. As *loka-pati*, God is the ruler of all worlds, realms, and states of consciousness. *Dhara-pati*, which is usually translated as Lord of the earth, also means that God is the ultimate (*pati*) support (*dhara*) of everything, as all objects are made of and exist in consciousness alone. This verse ends with calling God *Bhagavan*, the possessor of all glorious qualities such as wealth, fame, power, beauty, intelligence and renunciation, as well as *satam-pati*, the real master, guide and lover of righteous kings and humble devotees. It is to such a God that we beg for mercy.

The Good, the Bad and the Holy

भूयो नमः सद्वृजिनच्छिदेऽसताम्
असम्भवायाखिलसत्त्वमूर्तये ।
पुंसां पुनः पारमहंस्य आश्रमे
व्यवस्थितानाम् अनुमृग्यदाशुषे ॥

bhūyo namaḥ sad-vṛjina-cchide'satām
asambhavāyākhila-sattva-mūrtaye
puṁsāṁ punaḥ pāramahaṁsya āśrame
vyavasthitānām anumṛgya-dāśuṣe

We bow again to Him who rescues the virtuous from suffering, thwarts the growth of the unrighteous, whose form is complete purity and who grants the goal (Self-knowledge) to those following the way of the paramahamsas.

~ *Srimad Bhagavat Mahapurana* 2:4:13

Meditation upon Divinity frees us from impurity. Here sage Suta states this is because God's nature is Supreme Transcendental Purity Itself (*akhila-sattva-murti*). Contact with Him can bring only blessedness. The three categories of people mentioned in this verse are examples of how all benefit by contact with the Lord. The virtuous (*sat*) are those devotees who are struggling to live according to the dictates of the scriptures and the direction of the saints. Meditation upon the Lord frees such devotees from the suffering of mundane life by keeping their minds focused upon the source of all-happiness. The unrighteous (*asat*) are those who, identified with their bodies, egotistically try to satisfy their selfish desires without accepting any guidance or restriction. Their activities, although meant to bring happiness, ultimately lead to suffering for themselves and others. Meditation upon God changes their inner orientation and purifies their karmas. This impedes their future plans, which if allowed to fructify would only bind them in deeper darkness. The third category mentioned is the *paramahamsa*, the highest order of renounced ascetics who are completely free from identification with their body, mind and ego. Such sages are beyond all material contamination and are only intent upon the realization of the Self. The Lord grants such exalted souls the supreme boon of union with His pure being.

The Nature of the Soul

यत्कीर्तनं यत्स्मरणं यदीक्षणं
यद्वन्दनं यच्छ्रवणं यदर्हणम् ।
लोकस्य सद्यो विधुनोति कल्मषं
तस्मै सुभद्रश्रवसे नमो नमः ॥

yat-kīrtanaṁ yat-smaraṇaṁ yad-īkṣaṇaṁ
yad-vandanaṁ yac-chravaṇaṁ yad-arhaṇam
lokasya sadyo vidhunoti kalmaṣaṁ
tasmai subhadra-śravase namo namaḥ

We bow again and again to he who is known as the Divine Auspicious One, whom by praising, remembering, seeing, saluting, hearing about, and worshiping; immediately purifies men of the effects of sin.

~ *Srimad Bhagavat Mahapurana* 2:4:15

Love of God is the goal of life. But this love is not something artificial or external to our nature. This is because to love God is the nature of the soul. But the natural devotion in our heart is covered by the effects of lifetimes of selfish actions and their painful karmic consequences. This suffering often leads us to close our hearts even further, leading to more selfish action and their karmic results.

The only way to break this cycle is to focus the mind and heart on God, who is here called Subhadra, the center of abounding grace and benevolence. To do this, the main practices of bhakti yoga are outlined: singing, chanting and reciting God's names and glories (*kirtan*), remembering the name, form and activities of God (*smarana*), seeing the consecrated images of the Lord and the holy places associated with His manifested pastimes (*ikshana*), worshiping and offering prayers (*vandana*), hearing about the Lord from saints and devotees (*shravana*) and ritual worship, both at home and in temples (*arhana*). By focusing on God, we are purified and our natural devotion begins to manifest.

The Longing of the Soul

जयति जननिवासो देवकीजन्मवादो
यदुवरपरिषत् स्वैर् दोर्भिर् अस्यन्न् अधर्मम् ।
स्थिरचरवृजिनघ्रः सुस्मितश्रीमुखेन
व्रजपुरवनितानाम् वर्धयन् कामदेवम् ॥

*jayati jana-nivāso devakī-janma-vādo
yadu-vara-pariṣat svair dorbhir asyann adharmam
sthira-cara-vṛjina-ghnaḥ su-smita-śrī-mukhena
vraja-pura-vanitānām vardhayan kāma-devam*

Victory to the indweller and ultimate refuge of all beings, known as the son of Devaki, served by the heroes of the Yadu clan, who destroys unrighteousness and the misfortune of moving and non-moving beings with His strength, and whose beautiful smiling face increases the desires of the damsels of Vraja.

~ *Srimad Bhagavat Mahapurana* 10:90:48

This verse, spoken by the sage Suka, appears at the very end of the tenth book of the *Srimad Bhagavatam* which reveals the confidential activities of Krishna with His most intimate devotees, namely His family, community and the Gopis, the cowherd girls of Vrindavan. After hearing the beautiful story of the Lord, devotees may lament that Krishna lived His charming life long ago, and will feel dejected that He is not present before our vision here and now. But this verse is in the present tense. The object of devotion is immediately accessible. The manifest activities (*lila*) we have heard about are ever happening in the present. Krishna is victorious even now (*jayati*). The sage Shuka says that Krishna is "known as" or is "called" the son of Devaki (*devaki janma vada*), but in reality He is unborn and exists as the Self of all beings (*jana-nivasa*), whose realization removes all negativity and suffering. The verse ends with *vardhayan kama-deva* which means that He increases lust. We usually consider lust to be one of the major obstacles to spiritual advancement. But desire is a quality of the soul. The soul ever longs for union with its source. As we come from the Absolute Being, only the Absolute will satisfy us. It is this desire directed toward limited, imperfect and temporary objects that is an obstacle. Sadhana is meant to redirect our attraction to the One who can truly satisfy us. This desire for God is the secret lust that is at the heart of bhakti. The Gopis, whose story of unselfish love is told in the metaphoric language of romance, are held before us as the perfect examples of true and pure love for God.

7

Tradition

Gift of the Rishis

"Within the body exists all knowledge.
Within the body exist all gods.
Within the body exist all places of pilgrimage.
This can be attained through the teachings of the guru."

~ *Jnana Sankalini Tantra*

Tradition: Gift of the Rishis

Kaupina

Yogis, sadhus and brahmanas are known as *kaupina dharis* because they traditionally wear a loin-cloth (*kaupina*). Also known as *langoti*, *lingoti* and *komanan*, the kaupina is the symbol of discipline, simplicity, purity, freedom and spiritual culture. Wearing a kaupina controls the downward flow of prana and redirects it upward, awakening the dormant energy of the Mother Goddess knows as *kula-kundalini*, sleeping at the base of our being. This gives us the strength to practice austerities and to direct our attention beyond the body and its demands. The kaupina is an invaluable tool in the practice of sexual purity.

In Hindu culture, small children generally run around naked. But at puberty or at the time of their sacred thread ceremony (*upanayana samskar*), boys are taught by their mother or guru how to wear a kaupina and to regard all women, except their future wife, as mothers. From then on they are expected to wear a kaupina at all times as their underwear and to sleep, bathe and perform their daily spiritual practices wearing only a kaupina. As European fashion spread its influence into Indian culture, men began wearing shirts, trousers replaced *dhotis* and now, ready-made underwear is replacing the ancient kaupina.

It is important as yogis and devotees to resist the multi-billion-dollar undergarment industry's propaganda, and to continue to wear the traditional kaupina which is less expensive, more hygienic, better for health and more attractive. Scripture says, *kaupina purusha lakshanam* ("the loincloth is the auspicious mark of a man").

The Naked Yogi

दिगम्बराय दिव्याय दिव्यरूपधराय च ।
सदोदितपरब्रह्म दत्तात्रेय नमोऽस्तुते ॥

*digambarāya divyāya divya-rūpa-dharāya ca
sadodita-para-brahma dattātreya namo'stute*

Clad in sky, Your form shines with divinity.
You are the eternal Supreme Brahman.
Dattatreya, we bow to You.[1]

Our lineage is traced back to the primordial yogi Guru Dattatreya. The divine son of Atri Rishi and Devi Anusuya, Dattatreya was an *avadhuta*, one completely unfettered by social, religious or mental conditioning, immersed spontaneously in the Self. Dattatreya represents the mythic headwaters of the sadhu tradition. Many yogic, vedantic and tantric lineages trace their teachings and practices to Him.

Like Shiva, the Lord of Yogis, Dattatreya remains always naked, for nothing can cover His liberated consciousness. Traditionally, this naked-ness is an important feature of the sannyasi, for the *Paramahamsa-Parivrajaka Upanishad* states:

---

1 *Dattatreya Stotram, Narada Purana*, verse 8.

जातरूपधरश्चरेत् एश संन्यासः ॥

jāta-rūpa-dharaścaret eśa saṁnyāsaḥ

He should wear the form he had at birth. This is sannyasa.

In pre-modern times most sadhus lived completely naked in mountain caves or in forest ashrams, or they wandered homeless from place to place. The term for their nakedness is *digambara*, which literally means wearing the directions, and is often poetically translated as sky-clad. Digambara is not just being physically naked, but signifies being uncovered by ignorance, unidentified with matter, unencumbered by mental conditioning, and liberated from body consciousness. It is the symbol of the inherent state of naturalness, freedom, simplicity, detachment, and transcendence.

The Ochre Robes

In the *Srimad Bhagavatam* (XI:18:15) Sri Krishna describes to his nephew Uddhava the proper "dress" of an ascetic:

बिभृयाच् चेन् मुनिर् वासाः
कौपीनाच्छादनं परम् ।
त्यक्तं न दण्डपात्राभ्याम्
अन्यत् किञ्चिद् अनापदि ॥

bibhṛyāc cen munir vāsāḥ
kaupīnā-ccādanaṁ param
tyaktaṁ na daṇḍa-pātrābhyām
anyat kiñcid anāpadi

If a sage would have a covering, he can wear only a kaupina. He should not keep anything he has renounced other than a staff and bowl, unless in danger.

As part of the rite of renunciation (*sannyas diksha*), the disciple bathes in the holy river and unties his wearing cloth, allowing it and all his attachments to be swept away by the divine current. He steps out of the baptismal waters like a newborn child, without name to identify him or clothes to cover him, taking the first steps of his new life in his pristine and primordial state. The guru then calls him by a new name and presents him with a kaupina to wear when in mixed company. To protect himself from extreme weather and when interacting with the general public, a sadhu is traditionally allowed only two additional pieces of unstitched cloth, dyed orange in iron-rich mud. This is the color of the Mother Goddess, symbolic of the fire of renunciation. In modern times it is common for sadhus to expand this "bare minimum" to include other appropriate clothing, but the simplicity of remaining naked or wearing only a kaupina remains the ideal.

शून्यागारे समरसपूत-स्तिष्ठन्नेकः सुखमवधूतः ।
चरति हि नग्नस्त्यक्त्वा गर्वंविन्दति केवलमात्मनि सर्वम् ॥

śūnyāgāre samarasapūta-stisthannekaḥ
sukhamavadhūtaḥ
carati hi nagnastyaktvā garvaṁ vindati
kevalamātmani sarvam

The avadhuta alone, pure in evenness of feeling, abides happy in an empty dwelling place. Having renounced all, he moves about naked. He perceives everything as the non-dual Self.[2]

Dhuni: A Sadhu's Sacred Fire

The dhuni is a sadhu's sacred fire, passed down from Guru Dattatreya himself, through His ancient lineage of yogis and babas. It is the center of his universe. Although we sometimes perform Vedic or Tantric ceremonies in the dhuni, the dhuni is not the same as a Vedic fire altar (*havan kundh*). In a Vedic fire sacrifice, the fire acts as priest, taking our offerings to the gods, as is mentioned in the first mantra of *Rig Veda*, *agni mile purohitam*. In a sadhu's dhuni, the fire *is* divine awareness Itself, and not priest (*purohit*). The awareness of awareness burns all temporary names, forms, conventions, and attachments, reducing them to their fundamental reality: ash.

The dhuni is God, Self, kundalini and guru. The dhuni is the womb of the primordial Goddess. There

2 *Avadhuta Gita of Guru Dattatreya*, 1:73

are mantras for igniting the fire and the dhuni should not be extinguished. Beyond that no other rituals are necessary. The yogi lives, meditates, studies, cooks, sleeps and teaches in the light and smoke of his dhuni. The sacred ash is his medicine, clothes and medium for conveying blessings.

The Sacred Thread

Upanayana samskar marks the formal beginning of education into both secular and spiritual knowledge. Upanayana means drawing near to God. The ceremony marks the transition into adulthood, and is traditionally performed between age seven and seventeen. In modern times, this ceremony is only performed for boys from brahmin families. There is evidence that in ancient times it was more widely performed for both girls and boys. The ritual consists of worship of the family deities, offerings into the sacred fire, investiture with the sacred thread, and initiation into the holy Gayatri mantra by the father or guru.

The sacred thread, or *yajna-pavitra,* consists of three hand-spun cotton threads tied at the end with a special knot, and worn across the chest over the left shoulder and under the right arm. The three threads remind us of our debts and responsibilities to our parents, teachers and the ancient sages. They also represent three powers of the Divine Mother: Gayatri as Goddess of mind, Saraswati as Goddess of speech and Savitri as Goddess of action—helping us to become pure in mind, speech and body. More esoterically they represent the three subtle energy currents in the spine known as *ida, pingala* and *sushumna*, experienced by yogic adepts. Wearing the sacred thread marks one as reborn, and declares that one is mature enough to take responsibility as a full member of his family, society and religion.

The Gayatri Mantra

The most important aspect of the upanayana ceremony is initiation into the holy Gayatri mantra. Considered the Mother of the Vedas, this mantra is a universal non-sectarian prayer to the supreme divinity, shining *without* as the sun and *within* as the Self, to illuminate our minds and hearts. It is an invocation of the energy of intelligence, knowledge and love. The very sound of the mantra purifies karmas and grants divine experiences. The syllables of the mantra stimulate subtle energetic centers in our bodies, releasing physical, mental and spiritual potentials.

ॐ भूर् भुवः स्वः
तत् सवितुर् वरेण्यं
भर्गो देवस्य धीमहि
धियो योनः प्रचोदयात्

om bhūr bhuvaḥ svaḥ
tat savitur vareṇyaṁ
bhargo devasya dhīmahi
dhiyo yo naḥ pracodayāt

om = Brahman (the Absolute)
bhūr = earth plane
bhuvaḥ = heavenly plane
svaḥ = spiritual plane

tat = that
savitur = sun / Gayatri Devi
vareṇyaṁ = worshipful
bhargo = shining
devasya = divinely
dhīmahi = we meditate
dhiyo yonaḥ = our intellect
pracodayāt = illuminate

"Om has manifested as the earth, heavens and spiritual planes. That deity of the Sun, who is worshipful, who shines with divinity, upon Him (Her/It) we meditate. May our intelligence be illumined."

After receiving this mantra, the initiate is expected to repeat it prayerfully morning and evening throughout his life. This daily spiritual practice grants the inner strength to be truthful, noble, pure, studious, non-violent, gentle, firm, self-controlled, liberal and generous. The ancient sages teach that an aspirant who conducts himself in this manner will liberate his parents and ancestors from suffering and never fall from the path of God.

The following story is often told to young boys at the time of their initiation into the Gayatri mantra.

Once upon a time, there was a young man, born to brahmin parents, who lived a very sinful life. He would nightly visit the tavern and then enjoy himself in a house of ill repute. Early in the morning as the sun rose, he would leave the bed of women he didn't know, and go to the Ganga to take his bath. As he bathed, he would recite the Gayatri mantra facing the sun. Although he had no faith in this practice, he did it anyway because it was a family tradition. Every morning, as he was so bathing and chanting, he noticed an old woman washing filthy cloth in the river. After many months, it occurred to him to ask the old woman who she was and whose clothes she was washing. The woman then revealed Herself as the beautiful five-faced goddess, Gayatri Devi. She told him that the filthy cloth She was washing every morning represented the sins he committed the night before.

The Gayatri mantra is itself our Divine Mother, who by Her spiritual vibration, purifies us of all our impurities. But She can do more than that. If we struggle to live pure lives of devotion, She can reveal the light of lights, beyond all darkness, destroying our ignorance at its very root forever.

Brahmacharya

Brahmacharya means divine conduct—controlling lust by practicing celibacy when single and remaining faithful in marriage. Do not selfishly use the bodies of others nor misuse your own body through promiscuous behavior. There is a powerful divine energy within the body whose physical manifestation is the sexual fluid. Do not waste these fluids foolishly. Try rather to redirect them, as well as this energy, into higher channels by soul-elevating activities such as meditation, chanting, sacred study, self-inquiry, hatha yoga practice and dynamic selfless service. The sexual energies, impulses and fluids in the body and mind are divine. There is nothing bad or impure about them. The yogi strives to redirect the sexual energies, discipline the sexual impulses and preserve the sexual fluids. Our behavior should be restrained and respectful with members of the opposite sex. Immoderate sexual activity waste the sexual fluids, drain the nervous system, create deep mental impressions for sensual experience, and reinforce our identification with the physical body. Always dress, speak and behave modestly, refraining from pornography, sexual humor and language. It is imperative that we always seek refuge in the company of holy men and women.

Vedanta and Tantra

Vedanta, along with all forms of true religion, teaches that God is indeed within. Every effective school of religion must prescribe a viable form of sadhana. Within Vedanta, the primary methods are the cultivation of certain prerequisite virtues such as absence of anger, pride, envy, etc., as well as developing a strong desire for liberation. We must hear the truth about *Brahman* and *Atman* from the scriptures, and the guru. Then we must reflect deeply upon this truth, and meditate until we realize it ourselves. Along with this is the process of *neti neti*, negating all temporary phenomena to discover what is eternal and unchanging. This is a very difficult path. Actually, all sadhana is a struggle.

Tantra also prescribes its own forms of sadhana. Tantra is characterized by dynamic energetic methods meant to transform our consciousness. Primary among them are the recitation of mantras, the use of visualizations, hand mudras, pranayama, and ritual offerings. Some of these practices can be rather technical and complicated. Yet their true goal is the realization of the Self, through the conscious union of the individual soul and the Supreme Soul. Love, devotion and longing for God are fundamental in Tantra. Because Tantric practices are by nature and definition dynamic and powerful, it is imperative that they be performed correctly. The Tantric scriptures warn against making mistakes in practice. These warnings are aimed at those who practice in order to gain money, fame, power, or to harm others. The mantras, yantras and images of the Tantric tradition are manifestations of the Divine Mother Herself. To use them for selfish goals is itself the real danger. We must always keep the goal of God-realization shining brilliantly before us. Tantra is one of the many ways to help us purify our minds and hearts, develop real love and realize God.

This said, I feel it is my duty to share the real secret of spiritual life: *God's name and God are the same.* The chanting, singing, japa, and meditation of

God's all-powerful and purifying names are at the heart of all methods of sadhana. God's name is everything. Repeat it always and be blessed. Then we can be sure we are progressing in our search for the Divine Mother who dwells in the very core of our being.

8

The Seeds of Desire

"Attachment is the strongest block to realization.
This world is all attachment. Yet you get
worried because you are attached. If you are free
of attachment, you will lead a simple life in a
simple environment."

~ Baba Neem Karoli

The Seeds of Desire

Devotion (*bhakti*) and lust (*kama*) are both kinds of desire. We can say that they are two extremes of a continuum. At one end bhakti is a desire for union with the Absolute, and at the other end kama is the desire for selfish enjoyment. They both spring from the soul's fundamental hunger for spiritual completion. But while their source is one, their results are not the same. Bhakti, when fully realized, leads to the bliss of union, and kama, even when fulfilled, leads to loneliness and suffering.

Our guru Swami Vishnudevananda Saraswati used to tell us, "If you expect permanent and unlimited satisfaction from temporary and limited objects, you are bound to be frustrated." And frustrated we are.

Maharishi Patanjali says that the seeds of desire lay hidden and buried within the mind. They spring into life when exposed to the proper stimulus, either by proximity to the object of desire (temptation) or by the memory or imagination of the enjoyment of desire (fantasy). But not all the desires in our minds are bad, just like not all the seeds in the ground are bad.

We can see a correlation between the stimulus and speed of desires and their spiritual danger or value. A tree takes years to mature but brings blessings for generations; similarly the noble desire for righteousness, devotion, liberation, love, and service, which are awakened by holy company, grow slowly over years of practice, as we mature spiritually. A vegetable takes a few weeks to grow and satisfies our practical needs for sustenance; similarly the desire for food, safety, health, and companionship, which are awakened by the necessities of life in the body, grow quickly to keep us alive and thriving. But a weed springs up overnight and chokes the garden to death; similarly lust and greed, which flare up at the slightest stimulation, seem to consume the mind at the speed of thought and can choke our spiritual progress.

If a weed comes up, don't water it and it will wither and die. If we water it, then it will grow to maturity, choke out the healthy plants and then go to seed, thus making it even more difficult to resist the next time. How quickly we can lose control of our mental garden!

So this is sadhana. First, try to avoid the temptations that awaken the seeds of negative desire in the mind (bad company). This is not always possible, but we should try. Second, when a weed-like desire has awakened, don't act upon it—withdraw your energy. If we wait a bit, breathe, chant Ma's name, it will pass and we will be stronger. This is austerity (*tapasya*), for every time we overcome a desire, we light a blazing fire within that can burn up the other latent seeds before they have the opportunity to sprout. This is the negative aspect of sadhana. The positive aspect is the repeated planting of the Divine seed of Mother's all-powerful holy mantra deeper and deeper into our hearts and minds in meditation, and the constant watering of it by japa and prayer.

The secret is not just restraining the senses, but also in focusing on the Divine. Discipline and devotion must go together. The only reason we struggle to control our minds and overcome desires is out of love. We want to love purely, free from all selfishness.

Desires seem like they are coming from deep in the soil, especially for the big ones like lust. This is because lust has its source in the soul. We must "take it up to its root." We are bliss (*ananda*). We need ananda. We are seeking real pleasure, true satisfaction. We want union with the Beloved. But just now, through the trick of biology and our samskaras, we find ourselves trapped in body consciousness. This pure urge is directed to what we can easily get: physical pleasure. The frustrating part is that even the greatest physical pleasure is temporary, debilitating and binding, and thus ultimately disappointing. So let us tolerate a little burning and aim at what we really want.

9

Return to the Source

Excerpts from Letters to Devotees

"God is one's very own. It is the eternal relationship.
He is everyone's own. One realizes Him in proportion
to the intensity of one's feeling for Him. God cannot
be realized without love. Yes, sincere love."

~ Holy Mother Sri Sarada Devi

Return to the Source

Excerpts from Letters to Devotees

Divine Remembrance

God's name purifies the heart and mind, awakening love and longing for the Divine. The Divine Name can be sweetly rotating in your mind at all times, even amidst worldly duties. You should not wait until you have leisure for spiritual practice, for there is no guarantee that your free time will be spent in sadhana or that your spiritual hunger will increase. So now, while you have the desire for God, try to remember Him at all times. When you notice that you have forgotten, simply start the name and remembrance again. But do not feel bad about your lapse, rather rejoice in your remembrance! For the Lord says in the *Bhagavad Gita* that He is the source of both our forgetfulness and remembrance. What is required is our willing attention.

River of Bliss

Spiritual aspiration, hunger for God, is the most important blessing one can have. Spiritual hunger leads to sincere sadhana, and sincere sadhana leads to a progressive spiritual life. By regular repetition of the diksha mantras, our mind becomes more and more stable and a gradual transformation of consciousness unfolds. Japa is the foundation. Keep the current of Divine Remembrance flowing at all times. There is a river of rapturous bliss ever flowing just underneath our fluctuating thoughts. Sadhana allows us to feel, hear, see and bathe in this celestial stream. It flows in the center of our spine. It flows in the center of our being. It flows from the infinite ocean of *satchitananda* from which we come, in which we live and into which we will eventually return. The faint intuitive fragrance of this stream is love, happiness, joy and satisfaction. To drink from it directly is mind-blowing ecstasy. To drown in it is immortality, transcending the limitations of time, space and form in the Eternal One: the One we call Kali, the One we call Ramakrishna.

Building Bridges

When Lord Rama saw that the stones the monkeys threw into the water floated, he secretly dropped one into the sea to see what would happen. But his stone sank to the bottom with a plunk. A bit embarrassed, he tried again and again, but none of the stones he dropped floated. Hearing someone laughing, he turned around and saw Hanuman clapping his hands in joy. "How long have you been standing there?" Rama asked. Hanuman said, "Since you threw the first stone." Seeing the Lord's obvious displeasure, Hanuman said, "Do you know why the stones we throw into the water float? This is simple to understand. It is because we have written Your divine name upon them." Lord Rama then asked, "But am I not more powerful than my name? If my name can make stones float, then why did the stones I threw into the sea sink?" Hanuman replied, with his eyes now full of tears, "My Lord, anything that You let go of must sink."

A yogi is always watchful for pregnant moments when the external world reflects the internal landscape of sadhana, the inner goals of balance and rebirth, of being and becoming.

By following pure precepts we walk safely through Mother's realm.

Dignity

You are divine. Live up to it! Our frustration with our imperfections stems from our inherent perfection, and not from our supposed sinful nature. Our body and mind continually fluctuate and will continue to do so, as this is the nature of the body and mind. But we are not our body nor our mind. We are frustrated when we do not behave with dignity. So behave with dignity. This is sadhana. This is tapasya.

Remember that the three principles of a true spiritual life are service (*seva*), love (*prem*) and non-attachment (*tyag*). Dive deeper into Ma's name.

A Real Sadhu

Once an old sadhu died and went to the abode of death. Yamaraj, the Lord of Death, told him, "You have lived a divine life, so now please enter heaven." The sadhu said, "I will do as you direct, but I have heard many people talk about hell and have also read about it in the scriptures. It is my desire to visit hell as a tourist just to see what it is like. Will you allow me?" Yamaraj said, "You are most welcome to visit hell as a guest before entering heaven." The sadhu entered hell and took a nice tour of the main sights. Then returning to Yamaraj, he said, "Lord Yama, you have created such a wonderful realm! Hell is very beautiful!" Yamaraj, with much surprise asked, "How can hell be beautiful? Tell me what you saw there." The sadhu said, "I saw beautiful pristine forests, gorgeous palaces, breathtaking temples, fragrant flower gardens, devotees everywhere singing kirtan, gods and goddesses playing divine instruments and sages performing sacrifices. I felt the divine presence everywhere." Yamaraj then said, "Now I understand. You are a real sadhu!

Wherever you go, even in the depth of hell itself, you create heaven."

The AWESOME ONE stands Self-revealed between thoughts, beyond all dualities!

Everything Is Sadhana

God is arranging everything for us right now, this very moment. We're being set up. We're being spoon-fed situations. Every moment, every conversation, every interaction, every thought, every situation, every desire, every temptation, every experience, every penny—all this has been personally given to us for our spiritual development. Everything is either sadhana or a missed opportunity.

A yogi must know how to see the opportunity for sadhana in everything, an opportunity to become disciplined, simple, loving and free. This seems exhausting, but we are yogis—it's a full time job.

In the presence of the One, all duality is burnt to ash. And this ash is the ornament of the yogi.

Freedom From the Tyrant

Everything is an opportunity to see our attachment and to let go. When you feel the ego's hand gripping your throat, say the Mother's name and let go. Your letting go is the ego's letting go. Through this moment-by-moment sadhana, you will slowly gain the freedom to respond to everything with discipline, simplicity and love. Our soul cries for freedom from the tyrant, so our Divine Mother Kali comes through the guru and whispers Her most secret and intimate name into our ear, into our heart. When frightened by the tyrant and his weapons, we can whisper it back into HER ear and be safe.

With each invocation of the mantra, karmas change and grace floods our inner world.

The Way and the Goal

We are told, and we feel it to be true, that we need to purify our minds and control our senses. But we must remember that love is the goal. It is only through love that we can purify our minds and control the senses. Love is the only reason to do so, and love is the way to do so. If we think, "I will free myself from the attraction of sense pleasures," the idea of those pleasures is invoked and gets deeply rooted in the mind. When the appropriate stimulus comes along, they spring to the surface in full force. Whether pushing or pulling, we are still holding on. Instead we should "throw it to the other side" by affirming: "I shall delight in the glory of the Divine Mother; I shall see Ma in every situation; I will call to Her by name and hold Her in my heart." When the mind and heart are exclusively focused and filled with God in loving rapture, where then is the world and its allure? When there is only God, there is only God.

Recognize Your Goodness

You must recognize your goodness in your desire to be good. This desire to become a better person comes from the fact that we are all pure goodness in our essential nature. Thus your journey of self-discovery will lead to sweeter and sweeter levels of being. But my guru used to tell me that the way to heaven is often through hell. It is difficult to fight our habituated negative life patterns. Feel assured that the struggle you are going through has been experienced by everyone who has tried for an authentic mystical life.

Be patient with yourself and allow the mind and heart the space they need. Say the mantra. Let Her name be the line to hold onto during difficult times. Turn the japa mala. It helps. I promise.

Modern Disappointment

It is hard to deal with the disappointment that accompanies our expectations of sincere reciprocation. The loss of family cohesion and interpersonal connections seems to be symptomatic of the age. Everyone places themselves in the center of a shallow universe. It can be heartbreaking when we feel the ocean within but can't communicate or connect with those we love. My response is to place them all in Ma's hands and to live as deeply as we can. The awareness of depth can only come from regular sadhana. And sadhana comes from a sacred worldview steeped in deep sentiments and spiritual realities. It comes by grace alone.

Many a spiritual treasure lay hidden in pages of little known texts and in the minds of even less known sadhakas.

Close your eyes and see.

Om

All objects have their source in the eternal Subject. Some objects are far away, some are close to It. Mantras are near to It. Just like at Gangotri, it's easy to feel the source of the Ganga, because it's right there. Om is like the string of a mala—first we need to be conscious of the string *between* each bead, then of the string that is unseen *within* each bead. Lord Krishna says in the *Gita*, "Like beads on a string, all objects are strung on Me." Om precedes the mantra of each deity…Om is the string…Om is Gomukh.

My Guruji used to tell me that if you do not find God within your own Self, then you will not find God anywhere else. But only believing that the Divine is within is not enough. We need to realize this truth in our own experience. The striving that springs naturally from the yearning for this experience is called sadhana or spiritual practice.

In the fire of awareness, the yogi perceives the Limitless One whose blissful dance manifests this world of name and form.

The Perfect Gentle One, the source of Absolute Beauty, shines just behind our fluctuating thoughts. Still the mind and behold Him with loving adoration.

God's names and forms do not limit the infinite. God's names and forms reveal the infinite.

Rarefied Japa

In times of rarefied japa, consciousness is so clean that we are aware only of the subtlety of the mantra and aware of awareness itself. There is only perceiver and perceived—Shiva and Shakti. The play between these two is the secret of japa. There is a song in the *Kathamrita*[1] that hints at this:

> Sri Ramakrishna began to sing in his soul-enthralling voice:
>
> Tenderly, within the heart,
> Place our beloved Dark Mother.
> O, my mind, see to it that you see, and I see,
> But none else see Her.
> Lust and rest of them: elude them,

---

1 Authored by "M.", Sri Mahendranath Gupta, in 1904, *Sri Sri Ramakrishna Kathamrita* revealed Sri Ramakrishna's life and teachings to the world. This translation is by Swami Ambikananda Saraswati.

And come, O my mind,
Let us in seclusion behold Her;
Keep only the tongue,
That it may call out, "Mother!",
That from time to time, it may call out, "Mother!"
Wicked tastes and tellers of wicked notions:
Prevent them if they come close.
Place the eye of wisdom as a watchman,
And see to it that he remains on guard,
See to it that he remains ever on guard.

The mind will not always be in this state, but take full advantage of it when it is. We must be spiritual connoisseurs! When the mind is not in this subtle state, then constantly repeat the mantra with faith and loving attention.

The True Yogi

In this age of consumerism and commercialism kirtan has become performance, teachings and techniques are marketed as product and devotees are seen as customers. Now everything is done on stage and for a price. With self-justification that they are doing good, many disgrace their lineages and confuse and misguide the public.

The true yogi or sadhu, through his or her traditional life of renunciation and austerity, has the power to bless devotees, the integrity to guide the faithful and the authority to pass on the esoteric teachings of the lineage to a sincere disciple.

May the Lord of Yogis protect the sadhus in this dark age, as sacred speech is becoming polluted by the language of politics, entertainment and commercialism.

Workshops, concerts and tours—how far
we have fallen.

Making Sense of Our Sadhana

We sometimes get confused about what we are supposed to *do* in our spiritual life. We have ideas about what actions are spiritual and what actions are worldly. This causes confusion and guilt when we do not live up to our self-defined standards. But it is not what we do that is spiritual life, it is what we want. It is what we aim at. If loving and serving God is our aim, then this is the beginning of bhakti. Then we will try naturally to adjust our actions to attain our goal. Then our "work" will not be seen as material but as part of our spiritual lives, and any lapse in discipline will not be seen as failures but part of the struggle to obtain our lofty goal. The details of life become steps upon the path itself. The scriptural rules and regulations and our guru-guided disciplines are vitally important, but are not our spiritual goal—they are in service of our spiritual goal. Love is the goal. God is the goal. Pure love of God is the goal. The heart can never truly rest until this is attained. Only by keeping our focus on this can we make sense of our sadhana, justify our austerities and digest our shortcomings.

Secret Lust Behind True Devotion

There is something inside of us that both intuits the Infinite as well as longs for It. There is a throb within us that can never be satisfied living and dying within the narrow ruts of material culture, mental and physical habits and social conventions. We want to swallow the moon! We want to embrace the universe! That longing IS the soul. The soul is a verb. It is what happens to you when you fall madly in love with "The Beyond". Real religion is a desperate response to this painful urge. Always remember your own broken heart and its unreasonable need for the Absolute. This is the seed of spiritual aspiration. This is the fuel for sadhana. This is the secret lust behind true devotion to God. Be conscious of this and all the dilemmas that may and will come up can be understood and dealt with maturely.

It is important as spiritual aspirants to fill our minds with the sublime teachings of saints and sages who have realized the Goal. By their mercy our latent spiritual tendencies are awakened and new light is shed upon our own individual paths.

Always remember that there is no limit to our potential for self-delusion.

Trust your intuition—but not whimsically.

Voices of Sky

Living in a community of devotees and fellow aspirants is invaluable and precious, but not without its inherent dangers. I think a spiritual community should inform our world, not limit it, and help us see beyond our mental constructions, not build a fence around our mind. Only when you are away from the association of bhaktas and sadhaks, do you realize how the views of the outside world can limit us to an even greater degree by trapping us in conventional, artificial and materialistic thinking. The great sage Swami Rama Tirtha kept a diary which he called "Sightseeing from the Hilltop of Vedanta." As a teenager, this title really affected me. Our spiritual tradition, philosophy, practice and community are the sure foundation from which to behold the One beyond. Traveling can widen our world considerably. This is why the scriptures direct sannyasis to wander continually. Without this perspective, they would become functionaries and spokespersons of an institution, community or religion, instead of the voice of the sky (*gagana-siddhanta*).

She is much bigger than we can imagine. Remembering this helps put our thoughts in perspective.

Purity

From the purity of food comes purity of mind. Therefore please observe a strict vegetarian diet and refrain from mind-altering drugs. These items are extremely detrimental to spiritual consciousness, carry with them painful karmic reactions and make the mind unresponsive to the transforming effects of sadhana. They also open you up to negative energies and astral entities. Always purify your food by offering it to God before eating. If you want to purify your mind, you must simultaneously purify your life by always aspiring to live by the highest standards of humility, simplicity, etiquette and discipline. Never forget that your goal is pure love for the Divine Mother and say Her all-powerful name with every breath. Listen to Her name. Surrender to Her name. Take shelter of Her name.

Suffering and frustration may cause us to look up to heaven for succor, but by holy company we hear the Divine Voice calling us from above.

In the light of horrific events, as we look *out* with anger and justice, and *back* with compassion and remembrance, we must also look *upward* for spiritual understanding and deepening perspective.

Tightrope

You are a child of the rishis and heir to their inheritance. But spiritual life is not always easy. It is a tightrope act, the balance between tapasya and natural expression. At times we have to tighten up and at times we have to relax. "For everything there is a season." The same goes when you sit for meditation. When the mind is not still, then say the name with loving attention. Ma dances in the sound of Her name. And when the mind is still, then rest in the silence beyond articulation. Ma shines as still awareness. Both are the same. Sadhana is art, not technique. That said, it is still very helpful to do plenty of good old-fashioned japa throughout the day. The Tantras say: *Mananat-trayate iti mantrah* ("Mantra is that which frees the mind"). It is medicine for the mind. The japa mala can be a dear friend to get us through hard times. And then of course there is Ma. Trust that Her grace is upon you. I do.

While there seems to be many paths, really there is only one—the one you walk on. Every step reveals the path.

Shiva Shakti

This world is the ever-changing play of the Divine Mother. She manifests all this against the unchanging substratum of pure awareness. We must play our part in Her drama, but know that we ourselves are, in essence, that unchanging Self. This is the mystery of Shiva and Shakti. In the *Shvetashvatara Upanishad* (6:11) we find the mantra:

एको देवः सर्व-भूतेषु गूढः

eko devah sarva-bhuteshu gudhah
One divinity is hiding in all beings.

Patience and Trust

You sometimes get confused about your guru, ishta or mantra and your faith wavers. But it is not the guru or the ishta or the mantra that is the problem. It is the immature mind. A different guru, different ishta, different mantra—but same mind—same problem. Have faith in God and practice your sadhana with patience and trust. Remember how much the Divine Mother has shown you already, how much you have felt already. This is only the beginning.

Even in this imaginary world of delusion, there are signs reminding us of the unseen reality; markers of a forgotten geography.

Only Mother exists in this world. She is the Self of all. It is She whom you see with your eyes and it is She who sees through your eyes. She has become everything and everyone. To recognize this is to live in wonder. In the words of Dattatreya Avadhuta:

आत्मैव केवलं सर्व

ātmaiva kevalaṁ sarvaṁ[2]

Everything is verily only the atman (soul).

---

2 *Avadhuta Gita*, 1:4.

Notice the one eternal changeless Subject amidst the
changing objects.

By honoring the earth, we invoke the blessings of
Adya Prakriti, the Mother Goddess as the primordial matrix of all there is. May we, Her children, once
again remember how to treat and serve our Mother.

The Mystic

What is a mystic? Someone who wants God before
all other things. Not the God defined by religion, but
the God of the heart, shining as the soul of all beings.
Beliefs, dogmas and rules are not enough. The soul
of the mystic longs for union with the beloved who
hides in plain sight, simultaneously hidden and
revealed as everything and everyone. What keeps
us in seeming separation from the one being whose
heart beats the universe? It is ego, selfishness, fear
and separation. This is why the spiritual path is not
only joy and ecstasy, but also great struggle.

Do everything with dignity.

Inner Renunciation

We must constantly let go of our ego and its attachments. It is a great sadhana to be able to detach from our position or opinion on non-essentials, keeping the larger goal in focus. This is called inner renunciation. Only though this renunciation can we become truly attached to God.

Simple

Desire is not bad in and of itself. It is not wrong to want a successful and prosperous life. Just remember that real satisfaction comes from Self-knowledge in union with God. This comes from a life of devotion, meditation and service of others. As spiritual aspirants we are encouraged to keep our lives simple. This does not mean poor. It means simple.

The *Bhagavad Gita* teaches us not to be attached to the results of our actions. Letting go of expectations can be difficult. Then, work is transformed into worship.

A Deeper Japa

Ma Kali's name is Kali Herself, the Supreme Goddess, the divine Shakti that animates our lives and transforms us though Her love (*kripa*). But behind Her dynamic divine name and form, She exist as pure consciousness, the one transcendent ground of our very being—of every being. In the beginning of our practice, we struggle to keep the name in our mind, but gradually we should try to keep our mind in the name. This lighter "stance" can be a deeper japa.

This pilgrimage has taken this child along paths he could not imagine. The Master always looks for what His bhakta needs, not always what he wants. The Great Mother be praised! All great work proceeds this way. All must pass through the fire.

Daily Practice

Navaratri is a great time for inner transformation. The pujas and homas we are participating in are very powerful. But a thousand times more important than these special observances, is the regular daily practice of sadhana as prescribed by the guru. My advice on spiritual life to sincere devotees is to do japa and meditation on Ma's beautiful and all-powerful mantra, abstain from meat and intoxicants and to develop loving and selfless relationships with Her devotees. This is the work. This is how we progress.

Disciple Means Discipline

Our beloved Guruji, to whose feet I pray to be eternally attached, told me that *disciple* means discipline. One who follows someone's discipline is a disciple. This is what the word means. Yet this is not easy. Are we really disciples? I have always considered myself only an aspiring disciple. I want desperately to be a true devotee and disciple of Sri Guru and Sri Thakur. This desire is the core of sincerity and sincerity is our minimum qualification for spiritual life. The meeting of sincerity on the part of the disciple and mercy on the part of the guru is *diksha* or initiation. *Di* means divine and *ksha* means digest. This meeting is the beginning of the internalization of God-experience. Our appreciation of the mercy showered upon us compels us to respond in the only way we can, and that is through sincere practice. Our Guruji was always so pleased when he saw us practice.

We are already Hers. She is eternally ours.
Rest in this fact.

The question is not, "Have I seen God?", but, "Has God seen me?" We are only seeing God at all times, we just don't know it. But we should live in such a way that God will want to see us. This is revelation.

Sandhya

Equinox, solstice, sunrise, sunset, noon, and midnight—these are sacred and powerful junctures (*sandhya*) when the moon and sun, corresponding to *ida* and *pingala*, the lunar and solar currents in the body, are in balance. The yogi is a connoisseur of these pregnant moments, and by focusing his or her awareness at the center of this radiant stillness, can witness the dance of the One Beyond Thought.

The Inner Battle

The *Devi Mahatmyam* or *Chandi*, consists of seven hundred verses from the much larger *Markandeya Purana*. It is considered the main scripture of the Hindu Goddess tradition. It contains three mythic episodes of the Divine Mother's exploits told to a king and a merchant by an illumined sage. These ancient stories are told as a means to explain the nature of *maha-maya*, the mysterious power that causes our ignorance, attachment and bondage, but when recognized and adored as the Divine Mother Herself, leads to our spiritual illumination and final liberation. These stories are loaded with layer upon layer of philosophical, symbolic and mystical meaning. They record mythic cosmic events while simultaneously evoking corresponding personal inner transformations.

The gist of the stories is the repeated battle between gods and demons, the fundamental struggle between good and evil. In these stories, the demons get the upper hand and displace the gods from their heavenly realms. The gods invoke the Supreme Goddess, who is their own inner consciousness and power, to vanquish them. The scenes are sanguine and martial in nature, but the battles retold are symbolic of our internal struggles and correspond to the dynamic process of sadhana. The demons can be seen as representative of our baser inner enemies such as anger, greed, lust, envy, desire, selfishness, and ego. By invoking the assistance of our loving, yet fierce Mother, we are ultimately victorious over such lower energies.

Sri Ramakrishna said:

One must propitiate the Divine Mother, the primal energy, in order to obtain God's grace. It is She who deludes the world with Her illusion. We can go into the inner chamber only when She lets us pass through the door.

Be kind to yourself and trust in the purity of your aspiration. Trust in the real and lasting longing of your heart. Trust in the power of the divine name.

Burden of Grace

I am remembering my initiation into the sacred order of *sannyas*. I cannot express what it was like. Since that moment, I have felt the heavy burden of the Guru's grace. I beg one and all to mercifully overlook my many faults, and to pray that I bring glory to this most holy order by the service of Ma and Her children. It is only by the blessings of the devotees and sadhus that I can progress.

Viveka and Vichar

Viveka is distinguishing between what is permanent and what is temporary. *Vichar* is deep contemplation on the permanent. The only thing that is permanent is the experiencer; never the experienced. The highest form of vichar is meditation upon the Self. Ramana Maharshi explains: "Find out where from this 'I' springs from and merge at its source; that is tapas. Find out where from the sound of the mantra in japa rises up and merge there; that is tapas." In japa we think only the mantra, which is the manifest or vibrational form of the Self. When there are no thoughts other than the mantra, then we notice the space of silence between mantras. This space is the unmanifest Self, pure consciousness and the source from where all thoughts spring. If the only thought is mantra, then in the gap, where there is no mantra, there will be no thought—only consciousness. Through practice we can widen this gap and expand our experience of the experiencer. We *hear* Ma dance in Her name and *see* Her shine in the silence between Her names. This method is the essence of the last instruction our Guruji gave me while alive. As we become absorbed in this thoughtless consciousness, known in Tantra as the *bindhu*, we enter the *sushumna*.

We must bow to the wish of the Divine Mother, who always has our ultimate good in mind. Her ways are mysterious indeed and She is arranging everything for Her own purpose. She is *Icchamayi,* self-willed.

Maya is not an external power that tries to thwart our work like Satan (for which there is no equivalent in Hinduism). Maya is the delusive power of the Divine Mother, that, through our own ignorance and ego, makes the One appear as the many.

Gopi's Love

In the end the Gopis only want to please Krishna. Their all-consuming love is centered upon Him and His satisfaction. This is very different from our motivation. We love God because it brings us happiness and fulfills our inner needs. But the Gopis love Him because it brings *Him* happiness and fulfills *His* inner needs. Their love is 100% pure. This is called *shuddha-bhakti*. In the *Bhagavatam*, shuddha-bhakti is the real goal of life, not liberation (*moksha*) as commonly understood, which is still subtly selfish.

Prashad means mercy, grace and love. Everyone must feel nourished by Ma's love when serving, being served and eating prashad.

Shiva

Shiva is known as *Pashupatinath* and *Bhutanath*, the Lord of all beings. He exists in everyone you meet, seeing through all eyes, hearing through all ears. He is also *Yogeshwara*, the Lord of Yogis, and shines within when you struggle to practice sadhana. As *Kailashanath*, the Lord of the central mountain, He is the still center of your being. Your movements are His circumambulation when you stay conscious of the center. And He is *Adiguru*, the original teacher whose mercy lights the path to the pure and loving heart. May Lord Shiva guide and protect you as you wander the earth in His service.

Trishul

Shiva's trident is a divine weapon whose very presence protects us. *Trishula* means threefold suffering. The meaning of these three sufferings goes very deep. We are bound by the three gunas: sattva, rajas and tamas. These bring us pain from three sources: other people, nature and ourselves. These spring from the three worlds: physical, astral and heavenly. And all this comes from three fundamental causes: egoism (*avana*), actions (*karma*), illusion (*maya*). This leads to the three focuses of desire: property, sex and money.

Shiva is our deepest and most ancient consciousness. His trishul is His weapon of fire, whose three spears manifest as His three primary shaktis: Lakshmi, Saraswati and Durga. Above the central spoke resides Mahakali, the great void, the transcendental reality Herself, beyond even Shiva, beyond the Absolute Brahman. This is symbolized in Tantric imagery as the great cremation ground (*maha-smashana*). Touching Her, the three sufferings are burnt to ash: everything is burnt to ash. This is why we mark our bodies with three lines of ash (*tripura-tilaka*). When Shiva comes in contact with Mahakali, He lies naked in ecstasy, covered only in the ash of the world. Nothing survives the shock of God.

Sri Ramakrishna Paramahamsa, the great devotee of Goddess Kali, is considered the central force behind the spiritual awakening of this age. He and his consort, Holy Mother Sri Sarada Devi, are the male and female counterparts of the same divine incarnation. By invoking and honoring them, we are brought to the feet of the Divine Mother. Study regularly the words of Thakur Sri Ramakrishna, Holy Mother and Swami Vivekananda. They are safe, pure and reliable guides in this complicated age.

Her Seva

In this birth you have the treasure of the sacred mantra of the Great Mother. The mantra is a divine seed that will grow within and bless you with the fruit of Self-knowledge and God-realization. Utilize this birth for the service of others. Ma is present everywhere. She is the unseen power behind nature. She manifests in a great degree in human beings. Service to others is directly Her seva. She is the essence of your being. Repeating Her name awakens Her shakti within you.

Religious Consciousness

Religious consciousness is the intuition that there is something, or someone, behind or beyond everything. Religion is the reaction and expression of that intuition. But sometimes religion stifles, squelches or even kills this intuition. Some hold that people come to religion compelled by questions like: "Who am I?", "What happens after death?" For me religion begins with the intuition of the infinite.

Some modern scholars say that when a religious text is given a symbolic interpretation, it is a modern approach superimposed upon it. It is literalism, rather, that is the child of modernity. The ancients were superb at symbolism.

Attachment

We are attached to many things, but if we look truly, we will see that what we are really attached to is our self-image—to the way we want to be seen by others and to having things go the way we want. We are attached to being the center. Attachment is the main weapon in the hands of the ego. But the shining sword of detachment (*vairagya*) is the main weapon in the hand of our Divine Mother Kali. Put *Her* in the center and let the battle cry of our soul be: "Jai Ma! Victory to the Mother!"

Very Simple

Spiritual life is actually very simple: purify your body and mind by the yamas and niyamas, purify your heart by meditation on God's all-beautiful name, and live a clean life of love and service. This is ALL that needs to be practiced. When the mind and heart are pure, then love of God, the only reality, shines forth in and of itself.

Truly speaking, calling to Ma with yearning is not sadhana. It is the result of sadhana. Yearning for the Source is our nature.

I and Mine

I and *mine*—these always go together. They are the warp and woof of maya. *I* is the ego and *mine* is its attachment. Attachments are the support of the ego. If we remove attachment, the ego falls down.

If we deepen and internalize our consciousness, then the storms on the surface of life will not affect us so dramatically. They will come up, blow about a bit and then subside. This is their nature. In meditation we plunge into the depths so we can see how shallow the external world actually is. The external world will then lose its sting. Finally, it will loosen its pull. Then we will see the world with new eyes.

Listen Carefully

The living mantra given by the guru does the japa. The disciple only has to nurture the mantra, to listen to the divine name with care and attention. The sages say that the mantra is carved out of the heart. Ma is fully in Her name. We need to sit near Her and listen very carefully.

Our Sadhana is Simple

While we know, perform and teach elaborate rituals in the worship of Goddess Kali, our understanding and personal sadhana remains simple. We repeat Ma's name with sincere love and relate to Her as a child to its Mother. In this we are entirely followers of Thakur Sri Ramakrishna Paramahamsa and Holy Mother Sri Sarada Devi. They are our life and soul. At Thakur's and Ma's feet, the worship of Mother Kali becomes easy, pure and beautiful.

Love of God is your birthright.
Claim your inheritance.

With Ma's name we have everything we need.

It is through discipline that our devotion can soar freely without being lost.

We need to see through the eyes of love. We need to always see Her hand-feeding us at every moment and through every situation. If we were to see what is truly happening, we would live tear-soaked lives.

We are divine in nature. We should live up to it. When our Divine Mother sees Her children behaving with dignity, Her chest swells with pride.

Don't despair. You are Mother's child. Even in the midst of your spiritual struggles, Mother is holding you. Where can you go? You are Hers.